CAJUN CARNIVAL

American Myths and Radical Roots

Jennifer Cleland, Ph.D.

ISBN-13: 978-1475037043

ISBN-10: 147503704X

Library of Congress Copyright Catalog Registration
Number:

TX0004904416/1999-06-24

Front cover image: Pieter Bruegel, The Fight Between Carnival and Lent (1559).

Back cover image: © Peggy Haine (2010).

Author photo courtesy Cornell Photography

For my parents,

Robert Long Cleland

& Jean Thompson Cleland

ACKNOWLEDGMENTS

I would like to thank my graduate committee for their encouragement, especially my chair David Grossvogel for his unfailing patience and support. I first read Rabelais with him as a Cornell freshman in 1968. He always recognized my need to follow my own path, while offering a balanced perspective of my work and a good intuition of what I'm trying to say. Kathleen Perry Long was an invaluable help in my research and in revisions of this manuscript, and her courses on Rabelais and popular literature in early modern France inspired many aspects of this work. Marty Hatch enriched my graduate school experience through his guidance on issues of cultural identity and ethnicity, especially as explored through music, and was also a keen reader of my text, connecting it to relevant work by others and offering sound advice.

I could not have written this without the support of my parents, Bob and Jean Cleland, who have been brilliant role-models and staunch supporters. Finally, I want to thank my husband, Robert P. Stundtner and my son, Patrick Cleland Vittek for their love and their support of my work.

TABLE OF CONTENTS

INTRODUCTION

I have an early memory of a square dance near where I grew up in western Pennsylvania. There was a small acoustic band, including a fiddle and guitar as I recall, for the dancers in the dimly-lit barn; it's just one of many musical memories in a childhood filled with music, although most of it was classical. Despite that, I belong more to the tradition of square dancing. Most of my forebears arrived in that area north of Pittsburgh from Northern Ireland, some as early as the late sixteenth century. Known as Scotch-Irish, they were the immigrants most responsible for the importation of Celtic fiddle music to the Appalachian Mountains; along with the Afro-Americans who contributed the banjo, they created what is known as Bluegrass or Old-time music. Folk music was subsequently popularized by recordings and radio, and in the 1960's the folk music revival stirred further interest in the traditional tunes and songs.

As it turned out, I lived in Europe with my family during most of the sixties, spending four years in France. When I got a guitar at the age of fourteen, in Paris in 1965, I learned my folk songs from a Joan Baez songbook like most others of my generation. As a sophomore at Cornell in 1969, I profited from a solid course in music theory and lessons on the piano in preparation for a minor concentration in music. I left school, and classical music, to pursue a career in traditional music in the seventies. With the Highwoods Stringband, I traveled on three continents and played many of the major folk festivals in the U.S. Those eight years were a rich education in the traditional musical idioms of the world.

Back at Cornell as a graduate student in Romance Studies in 1990, I followed a line of research that was suggested by my experience as a performer of traditional music. During the seventies, the folklore establishment began to reject performers whose ethnic background was not considered sufficiently "pure", labeling them "revivalists". My band was summarily lumped into that category by the powers that be (and that sign the relatively lucrative performance contracts for government sponsored festivals and tours) with very little regard for our close associations with older, more "authentic", performers (or even for our own ethnicities, which were relatively coherent with the tradition we had espoused). The National Folk Festival went so far as to ban "revivalists" from appearing on their stages even when they were members of bands led by older, "authentic" players. In one case a compromise was reached when a fiddler from Indiana refused to play without his band: finally the band was allowed to play, but not to sing, not even their usual harmonies to the older man's vocals! Clearly this was a troubled policy, and many of us at the time wondered what would happen as we lost our musical mentors and became the older players ourselves. That question is far from resolved at this time.

The same questions of purity and authenticity haunt the broader discipline of cultural studies. In the traditional music world, older legends pass on, leaving those like myself who grew up with radio, television and an increasingly homogenized and commercialized culture. The subjects of cultural studies in general are inevitably products of the interaction between their inherited ethnic traditions and the mass culture that America, in particular, exports to the rest of the world. That is not traditional culture; when I discuss popular culture in this work, I mean the term to be understood as the traditions that develop from the bottom up in a society, not the mass culture that is often dictated by profit and in fact shapes the public's taste toward that end.

I had the pleasure of associating with a number of Cajun musicians in the course of my travels in the seventies. My group's most memorable trip was a six-week cultural exchange tour of Central and South America which included a Cajun band with whom we became friends, and later visited in southwestern Louisiana. The 1980's and 1990's have seen a surge in the popularity of Cajun food and music, cultural artifacts that reflect the original Acadians' exchange of foodways and other traditional practices like healing techniques with other residents of southwestern Louisiana, who arrived there from the Caribbean or Germany. My interest in their culture took me back to Cajun country as a graduate student, to experience and explore their Mardi Gras celebration.

While my own past has undoubtedly led to my choice of subjects for a thesis, Cajun culture is intriguing for many reasons, especially because of the embrace of multiple traditions that characterizes their culture. This is reflected in the fact that many younger Cajuns continue to expand upon their eclectic musical heritage, playing Cajun rock or Cajun blues; and of those who play traditional music who are Cajun themselves, some choose to play with people who are not, but rather have moved to Louisiana to learn the music. At the Festival Internationale in Lafayette, this year celebrating the 300th anniversary of a French presence in Louisiana, the only criterion in selecting prospective bands is that they sing in French: not only does the festival invite African and Caribbean groups, but the bands from Louisiana also have widely divergent styles. There seems to be no fear of the loss of "pure" Cajun culture, probably because it has been such a *mélange* from the outset; clearly the French language is the cultural boundary marker that defines the Cajuns' difference from the rest of American culture. However, the hybrid nature of Cajuns is often represented by Cajun folklorists as the assimilation of these other groups into a Cajun culture that has remained the same.

Folklore has been linked, historically, with nationalist movements, and as a result, with issues of racial purity. The Nazis themselves used this valorization of the "authentic" folk as an argument for ethnic cleansing. The politics of the folklore establishment has remained conservative; in the Appalachians in the early twentieth century, for example, English traditions like Morris dancing were taught to the mostly Scotch-Irish mountaineers, while African-influenced traditions that existed in the white community, like the banjo, were ignored by the people who promoted folk culture.

The Acadian Village in Lafayette, a theme park depicting the folkways of the ancestors of today's Cajuns, was constructed with faithful representations of the simple homes of the Acadians who regrouped in Louisiana in the mid-eighteenth century, after the *Grand Dérangement* when the British deported them from their settlements in what is now New Brunswick, Canada. As in Williamsburg, Virginia, the visitor is shown a slice of Acadian life as it was for the original emigrants from Canada; in fact, not all Cajuns lived this simple life for long. As time went by, their American experience shaped their lives: some stayed in the bayou and mingled with other ethnic groups, learning survival techniques from the Native Americans, sharing their own ritual magic traditions with the African-Americans, adopting the accordion for their *bals de maison*, and along the way creating the music and cuisine that is known as Cajun. Other Acadians became more affluent over time, and most of those took advantage of the system of slavery to accumulate property and wealth. As a result, Cajun society developed different classes. While a commercial venture like the Acadian Village has every right to popularize an image of simpler, happier days, all too often those who study Cajun culture seem to accept a simple, or rather selective view of what is considered to be "authentic" Cajun culture.

As is the general rule in folklore, poor people and outsiders are considered to have culture, while mainstream culture is seen as neutral by its insiders. Folklorists edit their interpretations of their subjects for the purpose of marketing it, if only to their colleagues; and Cajun folklorists seem to also seek to promote a rosy view of their society to the general public by ignoring its problems and focusing on its Old World exoticism. Their explanations of the Cajun experience in southwestern Louisiana seem to ring of the Acadian Village, where Cajun history is frozen in time and devoid of context, a Disneyesque representation of Cajuns designed for tourist consumption. It is culture packaged for sale, and devoid of controversy: with no Indian wars, no slavery, and none of the racial violence that was endemic in their region following the Civil War and into the twentieth century.

Yet this reflects the current climate of renewed pride in ethnic diversity; it was not always thus, and what some have called the Cajuns' reverse snobbery is the backlash of their historically second-class economic situation. In the early twentieth century, federal policies required every child in the U.S. to be taught in English; primary teachers from Québec to Louisiana taped the mouths of their francophone students shut to discourage the use of French. When that same generation of Cajuns fought in World War II, they became relatively integrated into the mainstream culture. Finally, the prosperity brought on by the oil boom of the sixties boosted the traditionally low self-esteem of Cajuns *vis-à-vis* the outside, anglophone world, and they realized that they had a unique and potentially lucrative cultural product on their hands. Folk customs have been promoted and reintroduced, and folklife centers have been built. Now that oil no longer provides the same level of income, tourism development is increasingly important for the area.

I applaud the efforts of Cajun entrepreneurs; the American public can benefit from lessons in cultural diversity and southwestern Louisiana can use the environmentally-friendly tourist dollars (Europeans flock there too). What I take issue with is the usual representation of Cajun culture, by those charged with disseminating its image, as primarily a product of their French extraction. What is lost in this distortion is the complexity of their unique, American experience, which parallels that of other residents of Louisiana, not that of their ancestors in France. Cajun Mardi Gras as well contains vestiges of the agricultural festivals that formed the basis of carnival in that era, but as it exists in the 1990's, Cajun Mardi Gras is an American phenomenon.

I searched the library for the roots of Cajun carnival traditions in early modern France and found an intriguing history of festive forms and the metamorphoses they experienced as the population moved from rural villages to towns and urban centers. The result of this transition was a loss of individual autonomy in general, but this was especially true for women, whose legal and property rights were abrogated during this period. The popular justice that was an important function of youth groups in the villages provided a model for the reassertion of traditional rights and privileges that accompanied the expanding power of the central government in France. As the population moved to urban areas in the wake of the wars and famines of the early modern era, society became more hierarchized and gender and class role-reversals became more prevalent themes of festive behavior. As conditions deteriorated for people in the cities, tax revolts borrowed practices from the *charivaris* of village life to fight the growing inequities imposed on them by the government in Paris to pay for the on-going wars. The interplay of the common people's expression of their ultimate uncontrollability and the attempts of the authorities to control their behavior characterized the carnival celebrations in urban France in the seventeenth century, as it does those in Rio de Janeiro and New Orleans in our own time.

My final chapter discusses the rich ambiguities of gender shading in the narratives of François Rabelais. Among the first generation of writers to use the vernacular, he was equally versed in classical literature and lore. His use of carnival and festive imagery to question the society of his day is a literary manifestation of carnival excess and role-play. Social role-play is central to his work; in a twist on Dante, the Pope in Rabelais' inferno sells green sauce. His stories feature some female trickster figures, notably the Sybil of Panzoult; yet critics have chosen to see him as misogynist. A truer reading of Rabelais would take him at his word and look for the marrow in his stories; he acknowledges the indeterminacy of meaning of perceptual reality and of texts, and thus invites multiple interpretations. Instances of androgyny in his narrative add further ambiguities: in a world of Andouilles, women from the waist up and sausages from the waist down, gender role-play is foregrounded.

Of course no one escaped Rabelais's satire, but the concept of the relativity of gender roles is central to issues of civil liberties, and hardly misogynist. A topsy-turvy reading of Rabelais reveals this aspect of his work.

Carnival is a reflection of, and specific to, the cultures that produce it; context means everything, and carnival is different things to different people. Carnival freedom gives rein to people's innate love of role-playing; more, it allows them to *be* the other, if only for the moment, and that leads to the awareness of the ultimately perceptual nature of reality that characterizes our modern age. Carnival is a many-faceted phenomenon; as such it offers a rich field for study, revealing tensions in a given culture. Peaceful or riotous, "rough music" or lynching, festive forms can release social pressure with the pop of a cork, or uncover the explosive power of the people.

CAJUN MARDI GRAS

It all began before dawn. The medieval-sounding Mardi Gras song, that had haunted the dance parties of the previous days and nights in Cajun country in both the black and white dance-halls, took over as the holiday's mantra. In the house where I was staying, the Balfa Frères' version of the Mardi Gras song started spinning before daylight to waken the household in time to drive from Lafayette, Louisiana to Acadia Parish, an hour away, to see a Cajun Mardi Gras run.

We first sighted the *course* that we would follow as a cloud of dust on a side road outside of Plaisance, a small village in southwestern Louisiana. The run had left the village at daybreak, and would make stops at many of the farmhouses on the backroads of their neighborhood before mid-afternoon, returning to town to celebrate with gumbo, a chicken and sausage stew served over rice, and dancing to a traditional band. The group of around twenty men on horseback, mostly young, some dressed in costumes of colorful satin suits, masks and conical hats, and some simply wearing ragged clothes and painted faces, stopped to regroup before approaching each house. Kept in line by their captain and co-captain, who were unmasked and wearing cowboy hats and satin capes, the group waited until their van with loudspeakers drove up to the house, playing a recording of the Mardi Gras song. Then at a signal from the captain, they charged the house, pulling up short before the extended family assembled in front of the door. For a while they performed tricks on horseback, dancing or standing on their heads on the saddle; meanwhile the "nègre," wearing blackface and a straw hat, acted as a liaison with the inhabitants. He approached the family asking them for "*charité*" (a contribution of food for the communal meal to be held that evening), and danced with one of the women. The climax of the ritual arrived when the man of the house released a live chicken, usually from the roof of the one-story structure; the bird often flew quite a long way before being captured, with gestures of triumph, by one of the riders. After the chicken was safely stowed in a pen on the beer-wagon, the entourage of riders, captains, and spectators following in cars moved on to the next farm to repeat the performance until mid-afternoon, when they would return to town for gumbo and a dance.

This scene, simultaneously occurring in many villages throughout Cajun country on Mardi Gras, has roots in francophone Louisiana that go back to the diaspora of the French settlers of "Acadie," now New Brunswick, who were expelled from their home in Canada by British forces and subsequently established themselves in southwestern Louisiana in the late eighteenth century. The practice died out for a few decades of the early twentieth century, due in part to the intense pressure for assimilation at this time, but also due to suppression because of the violent and uncontrollable nature the practice had assumed. It was revived in the nineteen fifties with some changes intended to make it safer, and with the participation of people old enough to have run Mardi Gras in the late nineteenth century.

The Cajun Mardi Gras begging tradition stems from the medieval *fête de la quémande*, with additional influences from the frontier heritage of the Louisiana prairies, such as the rodeo-style horseback performances.[1] In rural Cajun culture, as well as in the village society from which it derived, this tradition has its roots in a very basic need: the communal meal of Mardi Gras preceded the fasting of Lent, which in addition to providing a period of purification leading up to Easter also coincided with the usual end-of-winter food shortages of an agrarian society. The begging tradition allowed the community to pool its resources for one last good meal before Lent, requiring everyone to contribute something, as the Mardi Gras song says, "*même si c'est une patate et des gratons*" (even if it's a sweet potato and some pork rinds). These quêting traditions were a vital part of the social life of the culture from which the Acadians sprang. Sporting traditions were also important in early modern European New Year; springtime celebra-

---

[1] Barry Jean Ancelet. *"Capitaine, Voyage Ton Flag": The Traditional*

tions performed by youth groups included football matches and games which used chickens or other small animals as targets for arrows or rocks. The contest culminated in the election of the winner as King of the festivities. Later I'll explore these traditions in detail, tracing them from village to city.

Since the dietary restrictions of Lent are accompanied by taboos on drinking alcohol (and traditionally, sexual activity as well), Mardi Gras freedoms, like carnival celebrations elsewhere, give Cajuns a good excuse for a big party. Folklorist Ancelet stresses the connection between the "ritual" consumption of alcohol that is part of this Cajun rite of passage, and similar alterings of consciousness that accompany rites of passage in other cultures achieved through the use of hallucinogens, poisonous snake-bites or meditative techniques. The young men of the Mardi Gras, who typically must be at least eighteen to participate in the run, are freed as a result of the anonymity of the masking and the inebriated loosening of everyday inhibitions to be initiated into the adult world. Their experience of role-playing and mock trans-gressions such as charging a house, pretending to steal food or abduct women, feigning punishments (especially whippings), and sexual role-inversions like cross-dressing, constitute a rite of passage to adult life. In addition, younger children's experiences of these mock transgressions, which play off the psychological close-ness between fear and pleasure, reinforce feelings of personal and communal survival, as they learn to laugh at the scary masked men.

Historically, role-play (dressing and acting like "the Other") has been a staple ingredient of the carnival experience. As the population of France shifted from an agricultural to an urban arena, racial and sexual role-inversion emerged as important themes. In early modern Europe, sumptuary laws prohibited commoners to wear what are now the Mardi Gras colors of purple and gold (then symbolizing royalty) and red and green (then symbolizing the Church and clerics), prohibitions broken during carnival; these strict hierarchies led to intense play with class and gender images.

As Mardi Gras was introduced by European set-tlers into the New World, it was adapted by Africans to suit their celebratory needs. In the nineteenth century on plantations in the Caribbean, slaves dressed up in Euro-pean clothes and were wined and dined in the master's house at carnival time. More than fancy dress was in-volved; an observer in 1823 in Jamaica noted that "a perfect equality seemed to reign," so much so that "the slaves sang satirical philippics against their master, communicating a little free advice now and then."[2] In this case, the social distance between high and low was so great that "equality" for a day was enough, and actual role-reversal, though temporary, too radical a departure from the norm to be tolerated.

---

[2]Samuel Kinser. *Carnival, American Style*. Chicago: University of Chicago Press, 1990, p. 41.

Still, the role-playing by the slaves retains the ambivalence of carnival. As in present day New Orleans, the elite can afford to let the lower classes dress up and make fun of them one day out of the year, thus ensuring and propagating the status quo for the rest of the year, but at the same time providing the context for social change. More basically, parading costumed as Death, the Wildman, a bishop or the devil, disguises common in early modern towns and still frequently seen in New Orleans and among the Cajuns, people can play with their fear and laugh at it; this is the essence of carnival.

My initial experience of Mardi Gras in Cajun country left me with questions relating to the nature of their specific festive custom and its representation to the outside world by the larger Cajun community. Cajuns are famous for their propensity to *laissez les bons temps rouler;* like their fellow Celts, the Irish, they traditionally participate in a session of joke-telling at their wakes, literally laughing in the face of death, or even dancing with the corpse, as an affirmation of the continuation of life. As a springtime ritual, carnival affirms and celebrates the renewal of the natural world and the survival and regeneration of the group. This is the primary meaning of Cajun carnival. But I wondered, how much does Mardi Gras in Louisiana in the 1990's actually resemble early modern French carnival, and what does it tell us about contemporary Cajun culture?

I attended a lecture and slide-show by Barry Ancelet, folklorist at the University of Southwestern Louisiana, on my first visit to Lafayette. Intriguingly, many of his examples of Cajun Mardi Gras customs with medieval European antecedents involved women Mardi Gras participants. Most striking was a description of a modern enactment of *le Mort Ressuscité* (the Dead Man Revived), which Ancelet notes in his pamphlet was a play "once popular among the miracle players on the steps of medieval cathedrals. In this pre-Arthurian play, one participant feigns death and his companions 'revive' him by dropping wine or beer into his mouth" (*MG*,4).

Ancelet described an instance of a similar drama which took place during the women's run from the village of Iota, currently the only exclusively female Cajun Mardi Gras group. They wear Mardi Gras costumes and practice ritual behavior similar to the men. The women traditionally climb trees, and resist the efforts of the male captains to get them to come down. The woman in Ancelet's slide was "shot" down from a tree by the man who owned the property, who used a shotgun with blanks; after playing dead for a while, she was resuscitated with some beer administered by her colleagues. Ancelet noted that the image of the women in the trees with their colorful costumes reproduces ancient springtime rites of ornamenting trees to mimic, and thus attract, generative force. Fertility imagery can be also be seen in the masks worn by the women and men riders, who sport grotesque, phallic noses. But again, the nature of carnival is ambivalent; while these ancient elements of springtime rituals are well and truly present in Cajun Mardi Gras, the practice is also a reflection of the world the participants live in the rest of the year. Like carnival revelers everywhere, there is more than tradition to any given celebration; it is also play with and on a specific social environment.

I was intrigued enough by Ancelet's slides to visit Cajun country the next two years to follow the Iota women's run on the Saturday before Mardi Gras. The Iota, called Tee (Petit) Mamou, celebration, which is believed to have taken place continuously since the Acadians' arrival in Louisiana, is somewhat different from the equestrian runs of other towns. The Iota women run the Saturday before Mardi Gras; they ride in a wagon, rather than on horseback like most other groups, ostensibly because the community has gotten too spread out to cover by horse, but this also has the effect of making it a tamer event than some other runs. The Iota men ride in the same wagon on Mardi Gras day, with the same captain (whose wife is a runner) and co-captains. The women sing the same song, duplicate the men's actions of demanding charity and capturing chickens, perform mock abductions of children and make a practice

11

of mock attacks on male spectators (including folklor-ists) and captains.

The unique Iota Mardi Gras song has lines that are similar to lyrics of the *Gui Année* song still performed in francophone areas of Illinois, Missouri and Canada, according to a pamphlet distributed by the group.[3] This is a drinking song, and when I witnessed the Friday night rehearsal of the Iota women's group it was per-formed complete with a bottle of wine, which was drained to correspond to the verses: "Mardi Gras, quoi portes-tu...On porte que la bouteille...Et la bouteille est bue...Il reste que la demie (le plein verre, le demi verre), Il reste que la rinçure, et la rinçure on la boit pas!" this last accompanied by stomping of feet. The first verse, which asks "Les Mardi Gras àyou [d'où] viens-tu, Tout à l'entour du fond d'hiver?" (translated as "All around the end of winter" in the pamphlet, with a footnote that it

---

[3] *From France to Tee Mamou: Seven Hundred Years of Continuity and Change in a Traditional Begging Quest.* Pamphlet prepared by Rocky Sexton (1994) for Iota, LA.

"is sometimes understood as 'Tout à l'entour du fond du verre.'" or bottom of the glass). The next verse responds to the question: "On vient de l'Angleterre, o mon cher, o mon cher," interpreted as indicating that they come from far away. The next verses follow the draining of the bottle; the last verse, which is noted as being most similar to the *Gui Année* song, leaves little doubt about the fertility nature of the original custom:

> Bonjour le maître et la maitresse
> On vous demande un peu de chose
> On vous demande la fille ainée
> On va la faire faire une bonne chose
> On va la faire chauffer ses pieds!
> [shout]

The origins of this tradition have well-documented roots in European antiquity, adhering to the youth group and begging tradition which will be explored in the next chapter.

According to Carolyn Ware, who has studied the Iota women's run for years, it was started in the early seventies by a group of women whose families were active in the male Iota run, and has grown to include around thirty to forty women today.[4] The wagon, a converted cattle-trailer painted in Mardi Gras colors with "Tee Mamou" in big letters on the side, is big enough to hold several runners and a portable toilet. The captains ride in a pickup with an old chest freezer in the back full of beer and ice for the periodic beer stops. This is not random begging; clearly the people of the house expect them. When the wagon pulls into a yard, the women link arms in rows and march up to the door, singing their song without accompaniment. Then they dance with each other, members of the family, or one of the spectators. They have live music for this dancing, and the first year I followed the run I rode in the van with the musicians, young to middle-aged men who played fiddle, accordion and guitar. At each stop they played a Cajun waltz or two-step of their choice for dancing after the ritual performance. The next year there was a different group, with an older fiddler, but

---

[4]Carolyn Ware, "'I read the rules backward': Women, Symbolic Inversion, and the Cajun Mardi Gras Run". *Southern Folklore,* 52:2 (Lexington: University of Kentucky Press, 1995).

with the same instrumentation. Next they receive the donation of food or money, and if it's a chicken the chase is on through yards and fields.

The women work hard for their fun, whether capturing chickens or wrestling with the co-captains. Their play is more comical and less violent than in the typical male run; for example, they sometimes show their faces to small children who are frightened by their masks. They are endlessly creative in their play, poking around in people's sheds to find a tire to roll, a top or ball to play with, a broom to pretend to sweep with (and then ride), a mop to dance with, or a toy lawnmower to push around; if there is a ditch they might pretend to fish in it. They hide from the co-captains, who are charged with rounding them up to move to the next stop. Sometimes they climb trees and resist being pulled down, or try (and sometimes manage) to tackle the co-captains and steal their whips. All the women participate in the dancing and theater, but while a few of the Mardi Gras are self-appointed troublemakers, most of them don't make a point of confronting their male supervisors.

Cajun Mardi Gras in the nineties attracts media attention. When I followed the Iota women's run in 1993, the entourage assembled at the barn where they kept the wagon included folklorists Barry Ancelet and his guest for the weekend, Sam Kinser, and Carolyn Ware and myself, both graduate students at the time. There were also a reporter/photographer team from a major national newsmagazine and a video crew from a public television station in New Orleans. The local people, used to the attention (and interpretations) of folklorists, seemed more interested in their big day of fun than in what sort of spectator they attracted. The majority of the small group following the run were the husbands and children of the runners.

Although I only experienced the Iota women's run twice, my conversations with runners and impressions of the event led me to believe that what Mardi

Gras means depends a great deal on with whom you talk. This is confirmed by interviews that Carolyn Ware recorded with some of the core members of the women's run. In one interview, Gerald Frugé, the captain of both Iota teams, says that a lot of the play is predetermined theater. He says the co-captains can let the women get away with more than the men, and that it's "pretty to see a woman act up. Because it's easier to control the woman...over a man" (Ware, 148). He adds that "I don't mind when women tackle a captain. It gets the women excited that they were able to knock this man down, you know...It kind of livens the crowd up, gets everyone excited." His wife, a runner herself, agrees:

> When it's between the women and the men, when it...gets rough, what it looks like to the audience and what is really transpiring [is different]. The captain and the lady Mardi Gras have discussed it before: "You're gonna let me get the best of you and we're gonna put on this good show," you know. So to those looking on, it's real cute. (149)

There is no reason to doubt that this is true for her; but three of the most experienced performers joke together in another interview that "Gerald, he always tells us the rules. And we always break them...We shake our heads 'Yeah' and we go along with whatever he says, and then...Merline Bergeaux continues, 'I'm the first one to read the rules...[but] I read them backwards'"(148).

As much as Gerald Frugé characterizes the event as choreographed theater, one of the rowdiest members of the women's run experienced an encounter with a young captain very differently:

> During the day, he rolled over, and I
> mean my *capuchon* [conical headdress] –
> the cardboard, it was all torn up from him
> rolling over...I tackled him...And I had
> him in a scissors hold, and he couldn't hit
> me and he couldn't get loose. And you
> could hear him hollering, and calling
> to...[the other captains, who] just stood
> back and laughed...until he begged me to
> let him loose. (150)

This same woman told me that "This is the one day that we get the men back for all the shit we put up with the rest of the year"; moreover, her boyfriend bragged about how she had left a young captain "in a pool of blood on the dance floor." Although the captains try to limit alcohol consumption, their attempts are often circumvented. While Frugé's interpretation of the event seems to affirm the established social order of the community (men on top), the female woman runner sees her participation as a true challenge to social order, which although temporary, is still real at the time it is performed.

In fact, the women runners, although ostensibly presenting themselves as humble beggars, are also raiders of the home, the heart of the women's realm. As Carolyn Ware notes, "In their invasion of their host's household and yard, the women Mardi Gras symbolically challenge their own domain and by extension their traditional identification with the everyday norms of home, order, and respectability. At the same time, as Mardi Gras they claim access to wider spaces and to alternative roles in the social order...When Cajun women assume the role of Mardi Gras (one which typically suggests disorder and misrule), the powerful and disturbing image of the 'unruly woman' (Davis 1978:150) is foregrounded." (153). True, but the final act of the performance after the gumbo and the dance back in town indicates the ultimate affirmation of conventional social hierarchy: the captains drag the Mardi Gras, some of whom resist all the way, off the dance floor.

Not only do the captains have a different perspective on the event than the Mardi Gras, the women have different experiences among themselves. As one woman told me, "only the designated ones get hit"; all of the women know that the continuation of the practice depends on some sort of complicity with the rules, but some are dedicated to testing the limits. Ware concludes that, "although most Mardi Gras may 'push [he boundaries] a little bit,' as a captain says, those involved in the most transgressive play are typically those with reputations for such behavior in everyday life" (158); Mardi Gras roles may reflect real-world social roles in the case of particular runners, not just in the overall shape of the event.

These carnival festivities address universal features in human experience, the celebration of the natural cycles of life and the corresponding adolescent rites of passage, and the pleasure people take in the transgression of rules, and in playing the Other. Since the celebration of the return of the sun is common to all humans in temperate zones, this is no doubt the most important meaning of Cajun Mardi Gras. Still, there is another dimension to carnival, and, as Samuel Kinser points out, the mixed culture of the Americas requires more of a psycho-social analysis to understand more fully what the celebrations mean to the people who participate in them today. When I mentioned Kinser's book in my brief conversation with Barry Ancelet after his lecture, he expressed dissatisfaction with the way Kinser characterizes folklorists' interpretations of carnival. This is no surprise; Kinser maintains that there is *no* connection between ancient Roman festivals and European origins.

Further, Kinser states that "the folkloric explanation has done more to obscure than to clarify the meaning of the Gulf Coast celebration" (5).

According to Kinser, this obfuscation began when nineteenth century European folklorists

> recorded customs associated with spring-time plowing and planting which were carried out at Carnival-time...the form of these customs apparently had little to do with Lent or anything else Christian. These collectors therefore conjectured a pre-Christian rural origin for Carnival instead of a pre-Christian urban, Saturnalian one...Such a theory nicely supported the nationalistic ideologies of authentic "folk spirit" and anti-aristocratic populism sweeping Europe in the Romantic era when these ideas were elaborated...It now seems more likely that Carnival-time, beginning as an urban and courtly reaction to Lenten rules, gradually attracted to itself a variety of agricultural and social practices which were originally celebrated at different points in late winter and early springtime." (5)

This seems to be true of Cajun Mardi Gras which, as a *quête*, was not originally associated with Christian holidays, but rather with celebrations of the agricultural cycle, and was performed during winter and summer festivals as well as in early spring. The important point that Kinser makes is that Mardi Gras is not an ancient rural pagan rite that has been preserved for millenia; it is a living celebration whose character is fundamentally one of change and dynamism. He argues that even the ancient agricultural practices documented in nineteenth-century Europe that dated back to pre-Christian Celtic, Germanic or Roman nature-worship "had gone through an unknown number of transformations in the course of one thousand years of Christian and feudal-manorial history" (5). Cajun Mardi Gras is a contemporary phenomenon, one that doesn't dictate social customs to people, but instead evolves based on their situations and choices.

Yet Ancelet argues for unbroken traditions stretching from antiquity, for example showing slides of Iota women runners being mock-whipped by their captains for their transgressions, and relating this practice to the ancient Roman festival of Lupercalia, in which men dressed in animal skins whipped women to ensure their fertility in the coming year. Ancelet considers this a "remarkable survival of fertility symbolism" (*MG* 1); but it would be even more remarkable if this whipping had no modern contextual associations. It is too facile to describe Cajun Mardi Gras as simply the tradition-bearer of European traditions. In the revived tradition in Iota, for example, participants are required to wear special costumes, masks and conical hats that give the revelers a uniform appearance; this element of organized spectacle is borrowed from urban carnival. In a more significant departure from early modern practice, in which the youth groups had their own king for a day, the topsy-turvy world of Cajun Mardi Gras is subverted by the control exercised by the captains in this and in male Cajun runs.

While the Iota women wear unisex outfits, male Cajun runs often sport a few men in dresses and wigs. Cross-dressing in carnival has traditionally been interpreted by anthropologists as one of those rites of passage that lead to what Victor Turner calls a liminal state leading to *communitas*, the confirmation of the mutual identity of the group.[5] Caroline Bynum Walker argues that Turner's notion of role-inversion as part of the process of liminality is based on the perspective of the dominant class, and is thus specific to the dominant paradigm of normalcy. By liminality, Turner means a moment of suspension of normal rules and behavior to mark rituals of life-crisis or change; and he argues that images of status inversion often mark these liminal stages. Applying Turner's notions of the imagery of reversal and elevation to her work on later medieval piety, Walker finds that they "describe the stories and symbols of men better than those of women. Women's stories insofar as they can be discerned behind the tales told by male biographers are in fact less processual than men's; they don't have turning points. And when women recount their own lives,

---

[5] *The Anthropology of Experience*, ed. By Victor W. Turner and Edward M. Bruner. Urbana: University of Illinois, 1986.

the themes are less climax, conversion, reintegration and triumph, the liminality of reversal or elevation, than continuity."[6] Walker suggests that Turner's theory "may be based more than he is aware on the particular form of Christianity (with its strong emphasis on world denial and inversion of images) that has characterized elites in the western tradition--educated elites, aristocratic elites, male elites." She argues that by looking at women from the standpoint of the dominant (male) group, Turner

> in many places suggests that women are liminal or that women, as marginals, generate *communitas*...when Turner attempts to stand with the inferior, he assumes symmetry--that is, he assumes that the inferior are exactly the reverse of the superior. If the superior in society generate images of lowliness in liminality, the inferior will generate images of power...My research indicates that such things are very rare and that the images generated by the inferior are usually not reversals or elevations at all. Thus liminality itself - as fully

---

[6]Caroline Bynum Walker, "Holy Feast and Holy Fast" in *Anthropology and the Study of Religion*, eds. R.L. Moore & F.E. Reynolds. Chicago: Center for the Study of Religion, 1984, p. 108.

elaborated by Turner - may be less a universal moment of meaning needed by
human beings as they move through social
dramas than an escape for those who bear
the burdens and reap the benefits of a high
place in the social structure. (108-109)

Thus role reversal means something different for women than for men. For example, Walker argues that cross-dressing for women has been a means to change gender roles, as in the case of Jeanne d'Arc, or to make travel safer, whether for the purpose of a pilgrimage or an escape from husband and family; in contrast, cross-dressing was "a powerful and sometimes threatening image to the men who encountered it, so much so that they perhaps saw female cross-dressing where none existed" (112), since it questioned the very basis of male hegemony by positing the relativity of gender roles.

Walker notes psychological research that suggests that men's lives may be marked by the disruption in role-models that they experience as they move, as adolescents, from the world of their mothers to the world of their fathers, and that this may explain why women in general are less likely "to use images of role-reversal or to experience life-decisions as sharp ruptures" (114). In any event, cross-dressing has a political agenda; to wear clothing normally associated with, or in the case of early modern Europe, legally prescribed for, one or the other sex, is to call attention to the constructed nature of gender and to undermine claims about the essential nature of differences between male and female, issues which became part of the political landscape as gender roles were more structured in the urban environment.

In particular, gender inversions, whether in dress or in perceived social role, became more of a focus of the popular justice system, as gendered behavior became more codified and restricted in the urban setting. The *topos* of the topsy-turvy world gained importance as the traditional agricultural festival moved to the stratified society of the town. The division of gender roles was a reflection of a society that was becoming more codified in every way under the new order. This sort of vertical power structure creates pressures for those with authority, which raises the theoretical problem "that the dichotomy of structure and chaos, from which liminality or *communitas* is a release, is a special issue for elites, for those who in a special sense *are* the structures" (118); for women, Walker argues, that structure is largely irrelevant.

In *Vested Interests*, Marjory Garber's provocative study of transvestism, she notes that in the Renaissance, when dramatic roles for women were always played by men, "antitheatricalists, in their debates about gender, cross-dressing, and the stage, articulated deep-seated anxieties about the possibility that identity was not fixed, that there was no underlying 'self' at all, and that therefore identities had to be zealously and jealously safe-guarded."[7] The anxiety created by cross-dressing extended beyond individual sexuality; "Transvestism was located at the juncture of 'class' and 'gender', and increasingly through its agency gender and class were

[7]Marjorie Garber, *Vested Interests: cross-dressing and cultural anxiety*. New York: Routledge, 1997, p. 32.

revealed to be commutable, if not equivalent...The transvestite in this scenario is both terrifying and seductive precisely because s/he incarnates and emblamatizes the disruptive element that intervenes, signaling not just another category crisis, but — much more disquietingly — a crisis of 'category' itself" (32). She argues that the mere fact of reversability and artifactuality of gender roles throws into doubt the naturalness and manipulativity of gender roles (151), and notes the paradoxes evoked by cross-dressing. When powerful men belong to exclusive male clubs that feature cross-dressed members as entertainment, like Harvard's Hasty Pudding Theatricals or the Bohemian Club of San Francisco, "homoeroticism mixes with male-bonding...Far from under-cutting the power of the ruling elite, male cross-dressing rituals here seem often to serve as confirmations and expressions of it. Indeed, what is fascinating about the study of transvestism is precisely that it can occupy such contradictory social sites: stigmatized and outlawed in some circumstances, appropriated as a sign of privilege in others" (66). In Cajun Mardi Gras, male cross-dressing has this element of male bonding, complete with the exclusion and mockery of women that characterizes groups like the Hasty Puddings. The roots of this spectacle are in the urban carnival of early modern times, which were increasingly shaped by notions of a hierarchized society.

In Barry Ancelet's pamphlet, as well as in the lecture I attended during my initial trip to Cajun Mardi Gras, Ancelet has repeatedly expressed his concern about the way in which "outsiders" have interpreted the custom as a debauch with racist and sexist overtones. He argues that, "far from being a mindless and masked drunken frenzy, the Mardi Gras provides a quite serious context for symbolic expressive behavior" (MG, 2). Clearly a festivity as stylized and ritualized as this does provide a context for symbolic behavior; but questions remain concerning the hazards of a narrow interpretation of this ritual behavior as fundamentally a hold-over from early modern Europe. While the forms of the celebration may have remained faithful to (or been recreated along the lines of) their European antecedents, modern Cajun society, as I will try to show in subsequent chapters, does not have enough in common with medieval French society for the significance of these forms to remain static. If Mardi Gras is to mean anything important to Cajuns today other than as a tourist attraction, it will be in the context of their contemporary society; and it seems to me, admittedly very much an outsider, that there is a danger in overlooking the role that some of these festive forms play in propagating some values of Cajun culture which, in light of the civil rights and women's movements of the last half of this century, must be regarded as regressive at best.

Ancelet noted in his lecture that blackface in carnival festivities dates back to the Middle Ages, and he assigns a neutral value to this fact because of its relative antiquity. In fact, even that long ago, Aryans made up the ruling class in northern Europe, and medieval romances are full of descriptions of ideal beauty (blond hair and white skin) and ideal ugliness (dark hair and dark skin). The cultural Other is portrayed as mon-strous: a pamphlet from early modern France describes a Turkish "*monstre*" with horns and three eyes,[8] and an eighteenth century pamphlet tells (literally) far-fetched stories of "savages" in the New World.[9] The concept of the exotic Other is a trope integral to European culture, which blossomed after the "discovery" of the Americas; but to ignore, or deny, the racism implicit in this concept seems worse than naive. When considering the Mardi Gras practice of black-face in southwestern Louisiana in the 1990's, it is impossible to overlook the stringently racially segregated context in which it is performed. While my friends and I, all northern urban types, were tolerated in the Zydeco dance-halls where we went to listen to music, we were the only whites there; there was no sign of racial integration at the Cajun festivities. This is a society in which the Cajuns, as whites, are on top

---

[8]"Monstres prodigieux advenus en la Turquie": Jean de Bordeaux (Paris, 1624).

[9]"Histoire d'une Jeune Fille Suavage" (Paris: 1754).

even though some may be poor in relation to the rest of white American society.

It is easy to understand the appeal of the traditional folkloric approach to understanding Cajun Mardi Gras, criticized by Kinser, particularly to a scholar like Ancelet who is not only a folklorist but also a member of the cultural group he studies. Such an approach effectively relieves the group from the responsibility for the significance of their actions; but it fails to engage the researcher with the real issues. But when Cajun men dressed like a black couple for the Mardi Gras run are mock-whipped by the captains for pretending to be thieves, it is too close to reality, to the "official" world, to be interpreted as a carnival role-reversal; it reflects and maintains the hierarchy that has existed in this society since its transplantation to Louisiana.

While the relationship between the blacks, whites and Indians in this area is complicated by significant intermarriage and cultural borrowing, the democratic instincts of the original Acadian settlers never extended to other races. After the Civil War, slave rebellions were brutally suppressed by the Cajuns, with lynchings resembling the popular justice carried out elsewhere by vigilante groups[10]; the antecedent for this carnivalesque violence is the medieval *charivari*, in which youth groups enforced the social and marriage customs of their villages.

What seems more like carnival play than the Cajun's black-face is the white-face worn by black Cajuns in their Mardi Gras celebration, and Ancelet notes that white-face was worn in some cultures in Africa for ceremonies marking rites of passage, symbolizing the spirit world. But while the black Cajuns practice similar Mardi Gras runs, they do not include whipping rituals in their celebrations; presumably that would be too close to their historical experience for it to be fun. In fact, Ancelet mentioned in his lecture that one black man in white-

---

[10] Carl A. Brasseaux. *Acadian to Cajun: Transformation of a People, 1803-1877.* Jackson: University Press of Mississippi, 1992, p. 195-7.

face, who wore a clothespin on his nose to mimic Caucasian bone structure, insisted on removing it before having his photo taken.   Ancelet asserts that all the black-white role reversal is in good fun, and demonstrates a healthy knowledge of the Other; apparently on the part of this man, that knowledge included an understanding of the limits set even on carnival license (when it's being documented) by the realities of his society. Ancelet's far-fetched analogy of Cajun blackface with the African practice of painting faces white during periods of mourning demonstrates the tensions of his argument.

A claim that everything that happens during Mardi Gras is a remnant of Roman, or European, or even earlier Acadian traditions begs the questions, not only of why some things have changed, but more importantly of what Cajuns express about their perceptions of themselves and their world through these traditionally-inspired forms. In the Cajun ritual it is the more affluent members of the community who organize the Mardi Gras runs and act as captains. Since this is carnival, these are people laughing at their fears; the question becomes, what are their various fears? In addition, what are the cultural markers of their difference, and how important are these markers to the Cajuns' contemporary lifestyle, given that although some of the area's poorer inhabitants still live as trappers and fishers in the bayou, the vast majority of those who self-identify as Cajuns have embraced the amenities of twentieth century American culture? Does the history of Cajuns in Louisiana demonstrate close ties with France and things French, or is this predominantly a group forged from American experience?

These are the issues which led to my research into the cultures of the Cajuns, and of early modern France. The next chapter will trace the history of the Acadians in southwestern Louisiana, in an attempt to find insights into some of these questions.

MYTH-MAKING IN CAJUN COUNTRY

"*Vive la Difference*," proclaims a flyer distributed by the Lafayette Chamber of Commerce, and a similar product from Eunice, in the heart of Cajun Country, adds that this community has been selected by the University of Minnesota as one of the "Top 10 Cities in the U.S. for Cultural-Tourism Activities!" The Lafayette flyer claims that "Acadiana is a region unlike any other in the United States because everything here is accented by the French history and heritage of the area. Acadiana is proud of its past and especially of the fact that it forms a vital part of the present." The interplay of the past and the present creates culture; but I would argue that Acadiana is no more European than many other American subcultures, in spite of their retention of the French language. Instead, what makes Cajun culture unique and appealing is the rich cultural mingling that constitutes their American experience.

What distinguishes American from European popular culture? The folklorist Richard Dorson notes that "the circumstances of American birth and growth offer basic divergences from the customary evolution of cultures...Take away pagan divinities, chivalric aristocracy, an animistic universe, rigid and static societies, substitute physical mobility, social democracy, scientific explanations, and the historian finds reason for the different folklore expression of American civilization."[11] Dorson also points out that American folklorists, unlike their European counterparts, did little collecting in the nineteenth century, so printed material is virtually the only source of folklore in America prior to the twentieth century, and thus has had a greater than usual influence on American folklore than was true in Europe. Even the traditionally illiterate Cajuns' origin myth is derived in large part from Longfellow's poem *Evangeline*, itself based exclusively on literary sources.

Another investigator of American myths and legends, Richard Slotkin, believes that the Indian Wars of the early days of settlement were the definitve event of American history, the unique and formative national experience.[12] The Cajuns, both in Canada and in Loui-

---

[11]Richard M. Dorson. *American Folklore and the Historian*. Chicago, IL: University of Chicago Press, 1971, p. 174.

[12]Richard Slotkin, *Regeneration through Violence: The Mythology of the American Frontier 1600-1860*. Middletown, CT: Wesleyan University Press, 1973, p. 78.

siana, shared this history with the rest of Euro-Americans. The Indian Wars were a metaphor for the American experience, reducing the complexity of that experience to a simple contest between good and evil; in addition, says Slotkin, "part of the reason for its wide acceptance as a myth-metaphor derives from its recognition that the most significant peculiarity of the American environment was its substitution of racial and cultural divisions for the traditional English divisions of class and religion" (68). This was true for the Cajuns, who left their original land grants in Louisiana along the Mississippi River because of Indian attacks in that area; and, although the original Acadians' culture was relatively egalitarian within their own group, their relationship with the Native people in Canada and Louisiana was as hostile as most Europeans. Slotkin argues that the archetypal American hero is a figure of violence, a King of the Woods and of Misrule like the hunter Daniel Boone, whose love for and acculturation to the wilderness is manifested by violent acts against both the land and its original inhabitants; this thesis has resonance in Cajun culture. Patricia Rickels agrees that what she calls "a strong tradition of drunkenness, fighting, blood sports, and malicious practical jokes in the folk culture of male

Cajuns,"[13] which she believes is a result of their American historical experience, and "parallels the development of the American 'national character,' with its 'frontier psychology' and its emphasis on disorder, destruction, and violence...the image of New World culture as pastoral, orderly, Christian and sublime was a European invention with roots in the arcadian myth of the Greeks" (252). This myth was the basis for *Evangeline*, Longfellow's literary construction of Acadian culture; his source for much of its material was the writing of a French cleric, Abbé Guillaume Raynal, who traveled in the maritime provinces of Canada in the seventeenth century.

According to historian Carl Brasseaux, "Raynal, whose methodology was frequently faulty, had depicted the fiercely independent and anti-clerical frontiersmen as docile, priest-dominated peasants enjoying an idyllic, pastoral existence in an arcadian setting."[14] The pious heroine of Longfellow's tale was, of course, shaped by

---

[13]Patricia K. Rickels. *The Cajuns: Essays on Their History and Culture*, ed. by Glenn R. Conrad. Lafayette, IN: University of Southwestern Louisiana, 1978, p. 252.

[14]Carl A. Brasseaux. *In Search of Evangeline: Birth and Evolution of the Evangeline Myth*. Thibodaux, LA: Blue Heron Press, 1988.

the Victorian ideal of womanhood, but the male characters in the story are depicted as strangely passive as well, marching to the waiting ships for their deportation "with songs on their lips," praying to the Savior to "fill our hearts this day with strength and submission and patience!"[15] In fact, the Acadians' deportation was accomplished by force, after their own arms had been confiscated by English troops; and the life of Louisiana Cajuns also bore little resemblance to this portrait of pastoral tranquility.

In Search of Evangeline: Birth and Evolution of the Evangeline Myth is Carl Brasseaux's account of the Acadian image as developed in Longfellow's poem, in which he traces the evolution of the myth through time. Longfellow's story, originally viewed as a "thinly veiled historical saga," although fictional, was given credence by subsequent writers who, "interpreting these publications for the general public consistently used the fictional accounts of Evangeline as accurate historical narratives" (7). *Evangeline* was known throughout America, and it

---

[15]Henry Wadsworth Longfellow. *Evangeline, A Tale of Acadie.* Cambridge, MA: Houghton Mifflin, 1962, p. 54.

didn't take long for Cajuns to begin to turn that to their advantage.

The affluent Cajun Felix Voorhies rewrote the story of *Evangeline*, with a southwestern Louisiana focus. *Pouponne et Balthazar*, an 1888 novel written by Sidonie de la Houssaye represented Cajuns as crude and ignorant, reflecting the views of her social group, the Creoles, descendants of the exiled French nobility. In response, Voorheis wrote *Acadian Reminiscences: The True Story of Evangeline*, detailing the exodus of the Acadians as an inland journey through the Appalachians. He claimed that the story had been told to him by his grandmother, Emmeline Labiche, the true Evangeline; in fact, Voorheis' great-grandmother arrived in Louisiana by sea via St. Domingue (present-day Haiti), one of the stopping-off points for the Acadians deported from Halifax. According to Brasseaux, there is no evidence that any Acadians made the journey by land; all of them arrived in New Orleans on ships, from their various points of departure. Voorheis' fictitious account, like the odyssey in *Evangeline*, tells how the Acadians "crossed the mighty spine and wintered among the Indians" (21), reflecting characteristics of Slotkin's American hunter-hero.

Brasseaux argues that these writers, both in and out of Louisiana "inadvertently gave the Louisiana Acadians an origin myth, but a flawed one since it originated outside of the culture instead of developing within as the folks themselves sought self-definition" (7). Yet a quote from André Olivier, a member of the Louisiana historical society and a promoter of the veracity of the Evangeline myth in the form of the pseudo-historical figure Emmeline Labiche, suggests an additional element of fabrication: "The truth...is only this...that my land and my people are a myth. You may search for them forever and always you will find this is true...They are only an illusion, a myth of their own making" (5). The difference, of course, is that the image described by Olivier actually originates not from outside the region, but from outside the class which, for the value of its cultural currency, was marketed as early as the 1940's in Louisiana guidebooks.

Business interests originally provided the impetus for the promotion of the Evangeline myth, "transforming folklore into 'fakelore'" (8). Yet, says Brasseaux, as late as 1955 a history professor at the University of Southwestern Louisiana demonstrated an "uncritical acceptance" of the historicity of the Emmeline Labiche story (29); it is perhaps not surprising that the academy embraced the notion of the pastoral nature of the peasants, as well as that of the tragic heroine. In a classic American turn of events, the myth gained a visage when Delores Del Rio, the Mexican actress who played Evangeline in the 1929 Hollywood production of the story, paid for a statue to mark the purported grave of the tragic Acadian heroine in St. Martinville, and agreed that it be cast in her own likeness (41). It stands there today, and is featured on placemats and other memorabilia marketed in the area.

One thing that did not change in Voorheis' retelling of *Evangeline* is the basic plot, the separation of the lovers and the death of the female protagonist, reflecting the Victorian aesthetic which held the death of a beautiful woman to be the most poetic of subjects. Ironically, this dead woman became the only positive role model held out for Cajuns at a time when their cultural traditions were under siege, as official policies promoted assimilation by requiring universal education in English.

The history of the Cajun's acculturation in Louisiana, (like their expulsion from New Brunswick, and unlike the literary invention), is a typically violent story of the American frontier. Brasseaux details their early struggles with the successive colonial governments (first Spanish, then French) in New Orleans, and with the ecclesiastic authorities they sent to help keep the Cajuns in line. In many ways these struggles paralleled those of early modern French peasants with the emerging centralized powers there: the same bans on assembling in churchyards, the same clerical attempts to suppress the lay performance of Catholic rites by midwives, the same proscriptions against dancing during Lent that were imposed in France in the sixteenth and seventeenth centuries were rejected by the Cajuns in Louisiana in the late eighteenth century. Brasseaux records the "spirit of independence that characterized the Acadian response to the cultural imperialism of the immigrant [French] priests" (164), noting that "in seeking only minimal services and tolerating only minimal interference in return, the Acadians viewed the church in the same light as their civil government, and any action that deviated from their mental image of these institutions elicited a prompt negative response...Disputes over noecclesiastical matters usually deteriorated into violence" (165). Here again we see the American frontier ethos of the Cajuns; but these clashes also belong to the ongoing struggle between popular and official cultures of early modern (and our own) time.

While Slotkin's claim that violence is an American phenomenon seems to ignore its ubiquitous presence in human societies, American violence had an added dimension in pioneer days, when people living on the fringes of European influence really were beyond the arm of the law; and southern American society has yet another violent twist, the legacy of slavery. Brasseaux mentions that as early as 1785, 10 percent of Cajuns in the prairie settlements and 40 percent of those in the river settlements owned black slaves, although the average number was only six; while "control of the slave population was initially very mild...the presence of a large, alien, and subservient population by the 1780's nevertheless subjected the inexperienced slave owners to the constant specter of servile insurrection" (193). As a result of their fear of slave revolts, "both slaveholding and non-slaveholding Acadians...demonstrated no hesitation in mounting a united and openly hostile front against

threats, either real or perceived, from the slave community in subsequent years" (195). The growth of slavery
changed Cajun culture:

> Prior to the late eighteenth century, Aca-
> dians had consistently refused to recog-
> nize the innate racial, cultural, or social
> superiority of any group, while simultane-
> ously recognizing and abhorring the cul-
> tural and physical differences of their In-
> dian neighbors. This double standard was
> re-established in Louisiana following the
> Grand Dérangement, and ultimately ap-
> plied to the refugees' newly acquired black
> laborers...Thus, by 1810 what had been a
> nascent slave society had come of age.
> (197)

When the South lost the Civil War, the social unrest of
Reconstruction was slow to fade in Cajun country; and
although there are exceptions, *de facto* segregation of the
races remains the norm in southwestern Louisiana.

Class distinctions emerged as some of the Acadians took advantage of the upward economic mobility
that slaveholding made possible, while others adapted to
their environment by imitating cultural traits of Indians,
like Slotkin's archetypal American. Independent farmers
whose labor came from their immediate family, these

poorer Cajuns not only developed customs that helped them to survive in their new physical conditions, they also interacted with other poor people in the region, including ex-slaves, all of them creating a rich cultural mix. Ancelet presents these as the authentic Cajuns, who

> had the clear intention of reestablishing their shattered society in south Louisiana...though the outsider was welcome, materialistic values, strange customs, competitiveness, and a preoccupation with business, were not, at least among the poorer classes. Indeed, most Acadian yeomen and *petits habitants* flatly rejected American ideals, preferring instead their ancestors' precapitalistic values and folkways.[16]

Paradoxically, he paints a picture of Cajun culture as both pure and impure, as a cultural blend in which the whole is somehow less than the part he valorizes.

In a section about Cajun music, Ancelet mentions the social interaction between black and white musicians, noting that "descriptions of nineteenth-century

---

[16] Barry Jean Ancelet, Jay Edwards, and Glen Pitre. *Cajun Country*. Jackson, MS: University Press of Mississippi, 1991, p. 37.

dance bands had consistently mentioned Cajuns and black Creoles performing together. In the 1920s and 1930s, Dennis McGee performed and recorded regularly with black Creole accordianist and singer Amédé Ardoin. Together they improvised much of what was to become the core repertoire of Cajun music" (*C.C.* 151). While accurately crediting black Creoles for their contributions to Cajun music, this account paints too rosy a picture of the racial climate in which the cultural borrowing took place. Anne Savoy, who agrees that Ardoin "laid the groundwork for Cajun music as we know it today,"[17] tells us that "a vicious beating he received [at a *bal de maison*] is thought by most people to be the cause of his death." The crime for which he was punished? He accepted the offer, from the daughter of the house, of the use of her handkerchief to wipe the perspiration from his face.

Recently, Balfa Toujours, a group whose members include both Cajuns (notably Christine Balfa of the famous musical family) and transplanted Northerners (including her husband), invited a black musician and

---

[17] Anne Allen Savoy, *Cajun Music: A Reflection of a People*, Eunice, LA: Bluebird Press, 1984, p. 66.

friend to their show at a club in Basile, Christine's hometown; this gesture resulted in the cancellation of a future booking in the town. Christine, whose band has recently recorded with Amédé Ardoin's descendant Alphonse "Bois Sec" Ardoin, is quoted as saying of the incident, "It seems we can share the stage together all around the country and the world, yet we can't do it where we grew up."[18] While musicians routinely ignore cultural taboos against associating with members of different races and classes for practical as well as aesthetic reasons, society as a whole is slow to emulate their liberal views.

A recent work by a black Creole about traditional healers in her community (another folkway that demonstrates much borrowing among Blacks, Indians and Whites in the region) points out that

> The general attitude toward the emancipation of the Negro in 1865 was a bitter one. The race riot in St. Landry parish of that same year illustrates this. One account states that although the Whites of St. Landry condoned the defeat of slavery, they didn't want ex-slaves to rule them

---

[18] *The New York Times*, November 22, 1998.

(Dupre 1970). The general attitude of vigilante Whites then became one of malice, and a deliberate plan was devised to oppress Blacks to assure subservience. Their plan included the hanging of many early Black political leaders involved with issues centered around emancipation (DeLatte 1976).[19]

One is led to wonder about the connection between these vigilante groups and the traditional charivaris of early modern France: did the members of the White Leagues wear the masks and hoods of the rowdy Mardi Gras tradition, so similar to the costumes adopted by the Ku Klux Klan, to avoid recognition on these lynching raids?

We do know that the Klan used the traditional forms of the charivari (or "shivaree" as it is known in southern Indiana), in carrying out their popular justice. This custom was a method of social control, implemented by the youth groups in villages in all areas of western Europe. The targets of the "rough music", so-named because the rowdy bands played improvised instruments in front of the houses of their targets, were often people who had married inappropriately in the group's eyes.

---

[19]Wonda L. Fontenot. *Secret Doctors: Ethnomedicine of African Americans*. Westport, CT: Bergin and Garvey, 1994, p. 15.

Older men or women who had taken young spouses and thereby cheated the young people of prospective mates, and the town of the wedding feast (not required for second marriages), were ridiculed with bawdy verses until they consented to invite the crowd in for a drink. As we will see, the significance of the charivari (like that of carnivalesque traditions in general) has been fluid over time, itself changing to reflect the cultures that produce it.

The Ku Klux Klan, born in the mid-Southern hills of Tennessee and Indiana, originally enforced Protestant strictures against Catholic customs like dancing and drinking, duplicating the social proscriptions of the reformists of early modern Europe. As the organization spread to the South, Blacks (and specifically mixed-race marriages) became targets of its vindictive activity.[20] The Cajuns' sense of popular justice has remained strong; this connection can lend a disturbing subtext to the Cajun Mardi Gras riders' mock attacks on farmhouses, and to the begging and whipping of the

---

[20]Richard K. Tucker. *The Dragon and the Cross the Rise and Fall of the Ku Klux Klan in Middle America*. Hamdon, CT: Archon Books, 1991.

"Nègre". Whatever else it is, this sort of posturing is not carnivalesque role-reversal; like the actions of nineteenth-century Cajuns against Blacks, this seems more a continuation of the sort of "acculturation through violence" that Slotkin has identified as the archetypal American experience.

Ancelet et al discuss traditional "folk law" in Cajun country, including charivaris against marriages deemed inappropriate by the community. He notes that "violence was common throughout south Louisiana. The reasons were always the same: territoriality, isolation, a lack of civilizing influences, and a system of justice that did not necessarily include outside authority" (CC 105). Until the early twentieth century, "the main location for territorial behavior was the house dance and later the dance hall...Dances rarely passed without incident, because making trouble was a traditional form of amusement for some" (CC 105). Once the fight had been declared "official," no charges would be brought against either party. In fact, says Ancelet, this sort of fight is "not only tolerated, but expected and admired in certain segments of Cajun society" (109). The authors cite a study by Lynwood Montell which discusses "the difference between a killing and a murder in the popular mind: a murder is considered a crime, while a killing can be deemed an appropriate, although violent, resolution within the system of folk justice" (110). However, while including oral histories from the nineteenth-century of violence among Cajuns, they omit any reference to interracial violence. They also claim that it is easy to misunderstand the nature of the violence in the community, which is not random or gratuitous, since "people involved in violent situations usually know each other and understand why they are at odds...it is easy to see that what seems to make perfect sense on a warm Saturday night between two people who share a similar social and cultural background can take on other, more evil meanings when presented out of context" (110). But there are implications beyond this sort of "good old boys will be boys" justification.

This account of Cajun violence elides their history of white supremacy groups, although Brasseaux notes that most Cajuns belonged to these White Leagues during Reconstruction, and that "vigilante justice would remain a fact of everyday life along Bayou Teche and in the prairie parishes for another generation" (ATC, 148).

Violence feeds violence, of course, so fighting among Cajuns undoubtedly provided the context for attacks on Blacks. But it is worth recognizing the strained relationship between the races in southwestern Louisiana in any serious study of Cajun culture. The tendency of the ethnographers who come from within the Cajun group to put a positive spin on their legacy of violence reflects the self-consciousness of Cajun identity, especially now that their unique heritage has become a marketable product of interest to people outside the area.

A study of Henderson, Louisiana, self-proclaimed "crawfish capital of the world," reveals a grassroots element in the buying and selling of Cajun culture. Henderson was a fishing village at the edge of the swamp until Interstate 10 was built; then it became, not just the site of processing plants for the local fish and crawfish harvests, but, as Marjorie Esman's study shows, also a site of interpretation of Cajun culture for the tourists who stop by for a meal:

> Even the [restaurants] that don't cater explicitly to outsiders sell souvenirs to the occasional visitor who may stop in. Records of Cajun music are especially popular...other items sold include cookbooks

and handicrafts...In addition to selling souvenirs, the restaurants that cater to outsiders also provide other services to their customers that the locally oriented ones do not. These places informally interpret Cajun culture and history to their visitors, many of whom are unfamiliar with it.[21]

Esman notes differences between the restaurants catering to tourists and those more oriented toward the local clientele; local restaurants are casual and relaxed, and local residents typically use French in conversation with each other, although all but the oldest residents are bilingual (this may not be as true now as in 1985). The cuisine is spicier than in the tourist restaurants, where one will see more formal service with an English-speaking staff, pay higher prices, and eat Cajun dishes with toned-down seasonings. True to economic principles, the tourist restaurants give the people what they expect; by doing so, says Esman, "the restaurants protect the privacy of local residents while permitting them to share something of themselves and their culture with visitors" (36).

---

[21]Marjorie R. Esman. *Henderson Louisiana: Cultural Adaptation in a Cajun Community*. New York, NY: Holt, Rinehart and Winston, 1985, pp. 35-6.

.

In the past, the residents of Henderson considered themselves the "country cousins" of more citified Cajuns in Lafayette and other large towns. Esman theorizes that, since tourists are by nature transient (there was not even a motel in Henderson when Esman did her fieldwork), there is not time to establish a relationship with them, and so Henderson residents feel more comfortable with them than with more local visitors, who are aware of their perceived lower class status. Thus Henderson "welcomes outsiders whom it can control but is less enthusiastic about those it cannot" (125). According to Esman, giving tourists what they seek, and creating a marketable image of Cajun culture, "may require presenting a version of Henderson life that is not entirely accurate" (121). To cope with their changing conditions, Cajuns have been able to craft an identity that works to their benefit when presenting their culture to the outside world that comes in ever larger numbers to their door.

Interestingly, it is now more often the males, mostly self-employed locally, who use French as a "code language" learned at work, and spoken in the context of the fishing and hunting camp rather than at home with one's parents as used to be the case. Esman points out that it is also the men who typically cook the traditional dishes, often preparing the game and fish they catch. The women, in contrast, are now more likely to have jobs outside the home in the larger economy, and less likely to speak French than their husbands. Ancelet agrees that "it appears that the Cajun mother has been willing to give up her traditional language in order to provide a better education and life opportunities for her children" (75), producing what he calls the "rather ironic" situation in which men have become the transmitters of traditional culture. Yet as we will see in the next chapter, women already possessed an important degree of authority in the French villages from which the Cajuns emigrated, and they retained it in the move to the New World.

Cajun women were traditionally the repositories of communal folklore, and were often the primary healers in their communities. Male and female "traiteurs," or healers, continue to practice their techniques in Louisiana today, where they use the traditional Catholic prayers, complemented by herbal remedies they learned from the Indians and ritual practices, like tying knotted strings on the affected areas of patients, which stem from African tradition (Fontenot, 49). According to Carl Brasseaux, Cajun women were not only the transmitters of cultural values and religious instruction, but also, as late as the early twentieth century,

> served as unofficial 'deacons' of the sac-
> raments... Infants who could not be bap-
> tized by a priest were unofficially baptized
> by women in a ceremony referred to as an
> *andoyée*...Sometimes a priest was not able
> to visit remote rural areas for years, and
> this unofficial ceremony 'held' until the
> child was officially baptized by a priest
> and was especially valued when an in-
> fant's life was in danger before it had been
> [officially] baptized. (37)

In early modern France as well, midwives were author-ized to baptize infants who were considered at risk.

In addition to their spiritual and educational roles in Cajun society, Brasseaux notes that "Women's domi-nance over domestic affairs, always restricted by the husband's ultimate authority over family matters, be-came absolute on the death of the head of the house-hold," and the importance of women in Cajun society is "perhaps exemplified best by the fact that thirty-four of the ninety-one slaveholders in Ascension Parish (in the

1830 census) were widows" (42).   In addition to the measure of authority normally assumed by farmwives, typically partners in providing for the economic well-being of their families and participants in everyday decision-making with their husbands, Cajun women have often managed domestic affairs alone for significant periods of time when their husbands, fishers and trappers, or more recently oil-field workers, were away from home. Now Cajun women are more likely to hold jobs outside the home and less likely to be the tradition-bearers than their husbands.

Why then do Ancelet et al linger on what he admits to be an archaic model of woman as transmitter and guardian of Cajun culture? In their section "The Central Role of the Wife/Mother," they state that

> The Acadian mother was the principal
> means of transmitting and conserving
> Acadian values and culture. Considering
> the tiny size of the original Acadian popu-
> lation (fewer than four thousand), the
> fragmented nature of the immigration,
> and the enormous number of outsiders
> who have been assimilated into the Aca-
> dian way of life, the ability of the Acadian
> woman and mother to maintain and pre-
> serve the culture must be considered noth-

> ing short of miraculous...Wave upon
> wave of outsiders descended on the Aca-
> dian bayous and prairies. Yet, within on-
> ly a generation or two, most of these out-
> siders and their descendants had been ful-
> ly acculturated to Acadian ways. (69)

Yet these "Acadian ways" are neither agricultural methods or products, architectural styles, means of liveli-
hood, nor even foodways or music — all these are results of the *Acadians'* acculturation to their new environment; what remains is a strong sense of identity,
marked by a language difference, and artifacts like food
and music that are products of the entire cultural ecolo-
gy of southwestern Louisiana.

I would argue that while their language remained
French, the Cajun culture in Louisiana is more a product of American than European experience. While language remains a distinct feature of their culture, their
folkways adapted to the environment, quickly absorbing
features from other residents of the area, be they Creole
French planters or Indians. The cultural trait evoked by
Cajun "cultural activists" as the primary boundary
marker between Cajuns and the rest of the nation is the
French language. For example, the Acadiana Festival
which takes place each year in Lafayette features music

which ranges from Gulf Coast Rhythm and Blues to folksingers from France; the sole criterion is that the lyrics of the songs be in French. Yet even language issues in Acadiana have an ironic, distinctly American, aspect.

The use of French was dying out in Louisiana in the mid-twentieth century because of universal education and the proscription against speaking French in the public schools. Parents, also, used English with their children hoping to ensure the economic advantages of assimilation into the mainstream culture. When CODOFIL, the Council for the Development of French in Louisiana, was formed in the 1960's, however, the French that it promoted was not Cajun French; instead, apparently rejecting the hybrid nature of the actual usage of the area, they imported French and Canadians to teach French in the regional public schools, hoping to promote closer ties between Louisiana and the rest of the francophone world, and perhaps to raise the perceived lower-class status of Cajun culture. This action created a situation in which Cajuns study French for years in school, but, as one man complained, "still can't talk to Grandma." I would argue that this sort self-conscious cultural re-creation and manipulation for economic purposes is yet another reflection of the underlying American-ness of this culture.

Culture is not the same thing as identity; people continue to feel like a group in spite of changes in their environment, relying on cultural boundary markers which survive other changes to the group's situation. As Fredrik Barth argues, "ethnic distinctions do not depend on an absence of social interaction and acceptance, but are quite to the contrary often the very foundations on which embracing social systems are built."[22] Cajuns, while maintaining their ethnicity, do not hesitate to incorporate new cultural practices into their lifestyle. In Dewey Balfa's celebrated words, "A culture is carried out a generation at a time"; Cajun culture is dynamic, though respectful of its roots.

Brasseaux argues against the conventional claim that intermarriage resulted in the retention of Acadian culture, saying instead that "the cultural exchanges resulting from intermarriage gradually transformed the base culture, even in areas of Acadian demographic and cultural domination", and that even Cajun French,

---

[22] Fredrik Barth. *Ethnic Groups and Boundaries*. Boston, MA: Little, Brown and Co., 1969, pp. 9-10.

which by the early twentieth century had become the lingua franca of the lower classes in the prairie and bayou countries is "a linguistic hybrid including vocabulary drawn from Acadian French, Creole French, nineteenth century Standard French, and English" (ATC, 109). Nevertheless, the folklorists insist on the monolithic nature of Acadian culture, using surprisingly combative language: "How could Acadian women so easily subdue and dominate the culture of so many outsiders?" they ask.

They find the answer in the Cajuns' gregariousness. Now in the present tense, Ancelet asserts that "so strong is this ethic that Acadian culture assimilates the unwary outsider with considerable ease, almost deliberation, into almost every field of activity and sphere of social interaction" (71). It is difficult to tell if he is referring to the historically widespread intermarriage of Cajuns with other ethnic groups, or to the "unwary outsiders" who are courted by the marketers of "Cajun Country".

In a section called "The Role of the Male" (why not the "Husband/Father"?), Ancelet notes, again in the present tense, that "as in most families of European descent, the male is the head of the Acadian household and principal director of its economic and social destiny" (71). Not only was patriarchy not a particularly strong value in the villages of France from which the Acadians emigrated, Cajun men have throughout their history frequently been absent from home because of work in the fishing, trapping and oil industries; and Cajun women, because of their work outside of the home, play increasingly dominant roles. At the same time, Cajun traditions have been relegated to the domestic realm, and their language and customs restricted to domestic settings. As Marjorie Esman notes, "A child in Henderson learns that French is not appropriate for use on the outside and by extension that Cajun culture is appropriate in domestic and certain very restricted public contexts but not in dealing with the outside world or with strangers" (Esman, 51).

This domestication of Cajun traditions is linked to its commodification. Reducing culture to consumables like food and music recordings serves a double purpose for those who profit from this activity: not only does it encourage the production of saleable cultural artifacts, it does so by emasculating behavior which could threaten cultural tourism. The construction of the Cajun image belongs to a long tradition of misrepresentation and feminization of folk-life by the elite classes; the next chapter will consider the historical antecedents of the field of folklore, as well as newer, alternative models of cultural study.

DEFINING FOLK:

OFFICIAL REPRESENTATIONS OF POPULAR CULTURE

The essential problem of ethnography is the tendency to analyze ethnological observations in the abstract. This bias is evident in the work of the European folklorists who documented popular festive traditions. For example, the function of the charivari, which was wide-spread in western Europe at least through the eighteenth century, varied from time to time and from place to place, reflecting the political and social realities of the people who performed it. These conditions included the changing status of women, and attempts to accumulate large holdings by privatizing land traditionally reserved for communal use.[23] According to Edward Thompson, nineteenth-century folklorists, instead of studying folk customs in terms of their functions, sought to identify the common origin of those customs, which was presumed to

---

[23]Edward P. Thompson. "Rough Music": le Charivari Anglais" in *Annales: Economies, Sociétés, Civilisations,* 27 (mars-avril 1972), p. 307.

be a primitive Indo-European culture. This "evolution-ist" position seriously limited the value of their observa-tions: "C'est seulement lorsque la forme est réinsérée dans son contexte que sa signification sociale peut étre déga-gée, et que les ressemblances ou différences de fonctions peuvent apporter des éclaircissements" (292). Thompson uses Claude Lévi-Strauss's case study of charivaris to illustrate the problems of the classical approach to eth-nology.

Lévi-Strauss's opinion that remarriage was the cause of 92.5% of charivaris in France was based on his study of the results of a questionnaire distributed to *mairies* in France in 1937, by the secretary of the French Folklore Society. The study was intended to be used for an exposé of widowhood and remarriage customs to be given at an international folklore conference. However, the study specifically requested information on popular demonstrations against remarriage, and did not mention charivaris as such. Thompson cautions that with methods like this, "on se dirige vers une conception de plus en plus

abstraite, jusqu'au moment où la forme idéale--
maintenant fort éloignée des faits--se pose comme sou-
veraine envers le processus social et le remplace par une
logique poétique ou formelle...l'étonnant n'est donc pas
que 92,5% des réponses mentionnent le remariage
comme occasion de charivari, mais bien que le nombre
soit inférieur à 100%"(309-310). The results of this study
of remarriage customs in France supported Lévi-Strauss'
general theory that the exchange of women formed the
basis of human society, since the charivaris functioned to
censor practices which threatened the economic status
quo of marriage arrangements; yet the methodological
problems of the study render it inconclusive in regard to
the actual function of charivaris, the purported aim of the
research.

The generation of anthropologists which suc-
ceeded Lévi-Strauss was aware of the limitations of the
objectivism that he espoused. Clifford Geertz, a leading
inside critic of classic cultural studies theories, recognized
fifteen years ago that:

the effort to create a formal vocabulary of
analysis purged of all subjective reference,
the "ideal language" idea; and the claim to
moral neutrality and the Olympian view,
the "God's truth" idea--none of these can
prosper when explanation comes to be regarded as a matter of connecting action to
its sense rather than behavior to its determinants. The refiguration of social theory
represents, or will if it continues, a sea
change in our notion not so much of what
knowledge is but of what we want to
know.[24]

Another inside critic, Victor Turner, argued that "the
anthropological monograph is itself a rather rigid literary
genre which grew out of the notion that in the human
sciences reports must be modeled rather abjectly on
those of the natural sciences."[25] Turner notes that "Car-
tesian dualism has insisted on separating subject from

---

[24]Clifford Geetz, "Blurred Genres: the Refiguration of Social
Thought" in *Local Knowledge: Further Essays in Interpretive Anthropology*. New York: Basic Books, 1983, p. 34.

[25]Victor Turner, "Dramatic Ritual/Ritual Drama: Performative and
Reflexive Anthropology," in *From Ritual to Theater: The Human Seri-
ousness of Play*. New York: Performing Arts Journal Publications,
1982, p. 89.

object, us from them. It has, indeed, made voyeurs of Western man, exaggerating sight by macro- and micro-instrumentation, the better to learn the structures of the world with an 'eye' to its exploitation" (100). Yet, in spite of their recognition of the problematic nature of the methods of classic anthropology, neither of these scholars is ready to abandon the underlying project of the discipline as it has developed. Each of them retains a belief in underlying, explanatory principles of human behavior, capable of predicting pan-human actions, if only we could get them right.

For example, despite his "thick description" of social interactions among the Ndembu of east Africa, Turner's conclusion from his study of the Ndembu reproduces the classical ideal of an immutable behavioral law determining behavior: "Beneath all other conflicts in Ndembu society is the concealed opposition between men and women over descent and in the economic system."[26] The actual social dramas to which he had been witness, with their particular contexts of individual actors, are seemingly irresistibly reduced to a quasi-scientific axiom. By ignoring the specific context in his conclusion, Turner also reduces any perception of the human subjectivity of the object of his gaze.

In his discussion of ethnographic fieldwork, Clifford Geertz also recognizes that "this fact – that what we call our data are really our own constructions of other people's constructions of what they and their compatriots are up to – is obscured...it does lead to a view of anthropological research as rather more of an observational and rather less of an interpretive activity than it really is. Right down at the factual base, the hard rock, insofar as there is any, of the whole enterprise, we are already explicating: and worse, explicating explications."[27] Yet

---

[26] Victor Turner, *Schism and Continuity in an African Society*. Manchester: Manchester University Press, 1957, p. 89.

[27] Clifford Geetz, *The Interpretation of Cultures*. New York: Basic Books, 1973, p. 9.

Geertz also fails to escape the lure of the construction of social analysis as, ideally, a scientific enterprise whose goal is identifying empirical laws of human behavior.

Despite admitting "that there are a number of characteristics of cultural interpretation which make the theoretic development of it more than usually difficult," Geertz clings, with what seems almost a sense of nostalgia, to the belief that "there is no reason why the conceptual structure of a cultural interpretation should be any less formulable, and thus less susceptible to explicit canons of appraisal, than that of, say, a biological observation or a physical experiment" (24). Elsewhere, he states that "the road to the general, to the revelatory simplicities of science, lies through a concern with the particular, the circumstantial, the concrete, but a concern organized and directed in terms of the sort of theoretical analyses that I have touched on" (53). He insists that the ethnologist's "double task is to uncover the conceptual structures that inform our subjects' acts, the 'said' of social discourse, and to construct a system of analysis in whose terms what is generic to those structures, what belongs to them because they are what they are, will stand out against the other determinants of human behavior" (27). The problem with such a construction is the denial of the role that particular circumstances, and individual choices, play in the workings of society.

Renato Rosaldo proposes alternative models to social analysis. The central issue is the need to consider facts within their specific contexts, and Rosaldo suggests that the use of narrative, in which an individual describes his or her encounter with the object of cultural study in personal, specific terms, can be more valid, and more rewarding, than traditional methods of social study, since narrative can enrich social analysis by retaining contextual relationships which give meaning to cultural facts. Rosaldo argues that a more realistic approach to social analysis should focus on the "space between order and chaos," or as he calls it, "non-order" (102). Rather than attempting to explain people's behavior by formulating laws, we should "attend to improvisation, muddling through, and contingent events...even when they appear most subjective, thought and feeling are always culturally shaped and influenced by one's biography, social situation, and historical context" (103). Social life happens in time; one inherits some aspects of behavior from those who came before, and one contributes changes which affect those who will follow. Culture is a work in progress, not a set of rules which inexorably determines the behavior of individuals.

Rosaldo further asserts that, "in contrast with the classic view, which posits culture as a self-contained whole made up of coherent patterns, culture can arguably be conceived as a more porous array of intersections where distinct processes crisscross from within and beyond its borders" (20). This porosity contradicts the characterization of cultures other than the official culture of western Europe as internally homogenous and unchanging. According to Rosaldo, the ethnographer's "mask of innocence (or, as he puts it, his 'detached impartiality') barely concealed his ideological role in perpetuating the colonial control of 'distant' peoples and places" (30). Our modern experience of multiculturalism has reshaped cultural studies to reflect the conception of culture not as monolithic and static, but as experiential, fluid and contextual.

Rosaldo points out that anthropology has constructed culture as something that the cultural Other possesses, while the culture of the ethnologist is invisible, masking the interpretive and subjective aspects of ethnographic work, and that "using the 'detached observer' to make 'ourselves' invisible to ourselves has been debilitating" (198). Dismantling this sort of debilitating objectivism allows ethical concerns to play a role in cultural studies. By recognizing that the objects of our social analysis are also analyzing subjects with their own agendas, and by prioritizing their statements of what is going on in their own cultures rather than our interpretations of our observations, we not only get a truer understanding of our subjects, we also allow ourselves to be social critics as well as social analysts.

As an illustration of the politics which play an inevitable role in cultural studies I will consider the case of the Highland culture of Scotland. Malcolm Chapman argues that the historical context for the English construction of Celtic culture is the backlash of Romanticism against the Enlightenment ideal of rationality. Chapman notes that the eighteenth century was marked by the rise of industrial capitalism, and a demographic and social disruption similar to that created by the centralization of power during the early modern era in Europe. What we call Romanticism, perhaps the most significant intellectual trend of the eighteenth century, was a historically specific movement engendered by what was the very real tyranny of "fact" which had resulted in the sordid conditions associated with the burgeoning industrial capitalism of that time. Romanticism was constructed in opposition to the Enlightenment ideal of scientific and rational objectivity, and used nature as a metaphor for the morality which the Romantics found lacking in the their own culture:

at the same time as British intellectuals
were becoming more and more interested
in the nature of primitive man and primitive society, they had within their own national boundaries a fitting object for their
attention. The Scottish Gael fulfilled this
role of the "primitive", albeit one quickly
and savagely tamed, at a time when every
thinking man was turning towards such
subjects.[28]

The Highland Scots were close enough to the English to
be noticed, and different enough to seem exotic. Nature,
and by extension those cultures which were constructed
as natural, or primitive, were appropriated by the Romantics as "a source of and allegory for moral and ethical power" (65). Chapman finds it "remarkable how often the Celt is located in some kind of opposition to the
modern world, of rationality, economics, bureaucracy
and, as an image to stand for all of these, *machinery*,
which instantly conjures up an opposition of untroubled
nature, free from artifice" (105). He lists a summary of

---

[28] Malcom Chapman, *The Gaelic Vision in Scottish Culture.* London:
Croon Helm, 1978, p. 19.

the opposites associated with the construction of mainstream British and Celtic culture:

> intellectual/emotional, rational/intuitive, science/ religion, science/arts, externality/internality, instrumentality/creativity, practicality/sentimentality, culture/nature, materialism/idealism, objectivity/ subjectivity, artificial/spontaneous, society/family, modern/ancient, male/female, Anglo-Saxon/Celt. (106)

Though it appears near the bottom of Chapman's list, the basis of this opposition is gender difference, consistent with the Enlightenment construction of the female in opposition to the male. Thus, the Celtic character is constructed not only as primitive and natural, but as feminine.

Chapman notes that social anthropology, particularly since Lévi-Strauss' *La Pensée sauvage* (1962), has made much of the opposition of 'culture' to 'nature' which is found to be a very general feature of otherwise disparate cosmologies, and women are symbolically related to 'nature' within such systems (106). Chapman that the

equation of Celthood and femininity results in the conclusion that "they are alike in sentiment and feeling, rather than alike in political subjection and marginality"
(86). In fact, the Romantic mythologizing of Celtic culture could not occur until after the rising of 1745, led by
Bonny Prince Charlie, had been subdued, and any real
political threat to the English throne had been removed.
While historically, the nineteenth century would be a
time of integration in some degree into the mainstream
culture for many if not most of the Gaelic segment of
Scotland's population, the Romantic construction of "the
Celt" wished for a static, fixed and "unstructured unity"
(80), providing a suitable vehicle to validate the aesthetics
of the dominant intellectual discourse of the time.

The notion of race, language and culture as fixed
and mutually representative phenomena was an appealing construct for many students of culture even after Lévi-Strauss' structural anthropology began to make cracks
in the evolutionist edifice. Seeing their own society,
whether with pride or regret, as pragmatic and utilitarian,

theorists of society saw science and rationality as the end

point of evolution. At the same time, the

> "superstitions" of peasants and the work-
> ing class, the fancies of children, the my-
> thologies of antiquity, and the beliefs and
> rituals of savages were all conflated in this
> epistemological reduction. Models of
> mental development, like Frazer's compel-
> ling "magic to religion to science" (see J.
> Frazer, 1949, Chapter IV), carried the ap-
> peal of such theories well into the twenti-
> eth century. (114)

This confusion of the contemporary cultural Other with

the ancient culture of western Europe can be seen in the

Ossianic traits given to Native Americans in the work of

James Fenimore Cooper (47), and remains part of popu-

lar sociological discourse.

As anthropology is concerned with being per-

ceived as a male, "scientific" enterprise, folklore has

been perceived as the female side of cultural studies.

Chapman notes that folklore, as defined by F.G.

Thompson in 1966, "'is regarded as the knowledge of

former ways preserved by the inhabitants of the less-advanced countries of the world, and by the less-educated classes in industrialized countries'...the categorical requirements of folklore are, as we have seen, that it be survival, bygone, and simple-minded (or, to put it another way, pre-rational memories of former days and ways)" (121). Thus the concept that folklore is equivalent to ignorance is inherent in the academic discourse, and a world-view different from the rational empiricism of modern Europe must be reduced to a series of logical mistakes on the part of childish, and effeminate, people.

While anthropology has traditionally been concerned with the "primitive" abroad, folklore has been concerned with the "primitive within" (182); and modern folkloric study still has an affinity to the evolutionist school of anthropology, discredited among anthropologists themselves since the nineteenth century. The object of the folklorist's gaze is constructed as immutable; the criterion of "authenticity" in folklore is precisely this immutability, while any suggestion of the borderlands of culture, the living arena of actual persons in the Highlands of Scotland or in other locations isolated enough to retain strong traditions outside the mainstream culture, is denounced as inauthentic. Yet even Celtic folktales collected in the eighteenth century were informed by a contextual grammar, not just in terms of their renderings by the academics who collected them, but by the contemporary world in which their informants lived, as well as by the cultural intervention represented by the act of collection. The artifacts of folklore lose much of their meaning unless considered within this specific contextuality.

However, there is a more important issue: the attempt to "fix" cultures regarded as "folk," both in the sense of portraying them as immutable, and as the objects of benevolent efforts to help them on their way to rational empiricism, denies these people citizenship in the contemporary world. Again the question of what the ethnologist wants to know becomes an ethical issue, as the "preservation" of the culture of the Other can serve as a way to maintain the status quo to the disadvantage, in real terms, of the ethnic minority being studied.

The preservation of Cajun folk customs has been beneficial to a broad range of economic strata in southwestern Louisiana, and it has been accomplished with its potential for tourism in mind. Ancelet tells us that throughout the nineteenth and early twentieth centuries, the *course de Mardi Gras* could be found in most areas of French Louisiana from the Mississippi River to Texas, and that it was "characterized by a mystique of toughness reminiscent of the days of the American Wild West. The anonymity of the masked riders provided an ideal reckoning ground for quarreling parties. In earlier times scores were often settled on this day with bare fists, knives and even pistols...With the arrival of Americanization and the 'civilizing' effect of new schools and churches, however, the often rowdy celebration was banned from many communities" (MG 4). When the custom was revived in the fifties, not only was it made an exclusively male ritual, the revivalists "took great pains to render the celebration respectable and relatively safe for both riders and hosts" (MG 6). The captains of the revived Mardi Gras runs are civic and church leaders in the community, who arrange stops at the more affluent farmsteads in their communities; clearly, while the form of the celebration recalls archaic French begging rituals, there is considerable effort made to control the expression of the popular will to avoid any real threat to the accessibility of the festivities to outsiders.

As Kinser asserts, Mardi Gras on the Gulf Coast is dynamic, and a reflection of the changing times, although there are continuities and parallels with older and other examples of carnival:

> If the racial, sexual, and economic barriers
> in a community are represented as hazy
> walls or low and flimsy barriers during
> Carnival--as in the transvestism of street
> maskers and the willing largesse of the
> float dukes--then one can wager that the
> organizers of the representation imagine
> them and then indeed act as if they are
> pretty high, hard walls the rest of the year.
> If they are represented as hard walls and

indelible differences during the festival--
like the boastful supremacies of the black
Indian tribes and the imperturbable gran-
deur of the pseudo-kings--then one may
guess that they look to the organizers as if
they are unstable in actuality, in need of
shoring up, refurbishment, and everyday
attention. (318)

Is the representation of racial and sexual boundaries in
Cajun Mardi Gras as high and hard a sign that the traditional white male supremacy is perceived as threatened
by current changes in Cajun society? What is the motivation for refuting this threat, not just for Cajuns, but for
those who represent Cajun culture to the world?

The most obvious answer is, a lot of tourist reve-
nue; and, now that the oil boom in their region has gone
"bust," that income is more important than ever. It is
economically sound for the political and economic leaders of the region to promote a Cajun culture which is
stable, cohesive, and most importantly, different from
mainstream America. One writer calls Cajuns "the pets
of Louisiana, fondly portrayed with just a hint of ridicule;" adding that while "the stereotype of Cajuns as

people who spend their time drinking beer and telling stories in a quaint accent has been just as damaging to Cajun cultural pride as the older ban against speaking French in the classroom...The Cajuns have now begun to transform mockery into a weapon of their own, in the spirit of ethnic revival. They boast about their beer drinking, fast driving, and quick fists."[29] In the same vein, Marjorie Esman says that some of the young Cajun men take "an arrogant pride in their heritage and in the fact that they share a tradition different from that of the U.S. majority. They relish the reputation Cajuns have acquired as a rough and wild people. To this group, proficiency in French is a sign of prestige, a kind of reverse snobbery that glorifies a stigma" (53). There are echoes of what Esman calls this "reverse snobbery" in Ancelet's assessment of the frontier values of the Cajuns: "Friendly, yet suspicious of strangers; easy-going, yet stubborn; deeply religious, yet anti-clerical; proud, yet quick to laugh at their own foibles; unfailingly loyal,

---

[29] Christopher Hallowell. *People of the Bayou: Cajun Life in Lost America*. New York: E.P. Dutton, 1979, p. 74.

yet possessed of a frontier independence--Cajuns are immediately recognizable as a people, yet defy facile definition. As the saying goes, 'You can tell a Cajun a mile away, but you can't tell him a damn thing up close" (*CC*, xvii). Sounding a bit defensive about the assimilation that is the overwhelming feature of Cajun culture, Ancelet insists that "such change may even be a sign of vitality. People have been predicting the demise of Cajun culture for decades. Yet every time someone tries to pronounce a funeral oration, the corpse sits up in the coffin" (CC xviii). Again, it seems more accurate to argue the survival of the Cajuns as a self-recognized group, rather than the survival of discrete cultural characteristics predating their acculturation to southwestern Louisiana.

In fact, Ancelet's praise of the survival of the Cajuns as a group reflects the internalization, at least by upper-class Cajuns, of that most American of values, the drive for success. While paying lip service to the complexity of Cajun culture, he works hard to promote a view of the group as monolithic and domesticated, for the apparent purpose of promoting the culture. Cajuns are represented as an American success story, in which cultural borrowing and exchange has provided

> an enormously successful springboard for what has appeared to some in the outside world as a miraculous Cinderella-type transformation: from brute peasant to so-phisticated beared of a rich and fascinat-ing set of alternate American traditions, all in a handful of generations. (*CC*, 229)

While acculturation is credited with the survival of the group's values, those values are presented as paradoxi-cally monolithic and fixed in opposition to the rest of the cultural traits of the group, since although Cajuns have diverse lifestyles, each of them "also carries something of the lifeways and values described in this book" (*CC*, 230). Yet, as we have seen, values like the egalitarian-ism of the original Acadian settlers changed quickly when faced with the realities of the New World. This representation of Cajun values as static is the ongoing invention of those with a stake in the appeal that this group has for cultural tourism: the Cajuns should seem unique, and different from (but not threatening to) mainstream America; and should continue to walk that fine line, successfully. In contrast, Brasseaux notes that the post-bellum "Acadian gentry made every effort to disassociate themselves from their heritage and, concomitantly, their poor relations, by wrapping themselves in the ennobling mantle of the Evangeline legend and ultimately identifying themselves as 'American'" (ATC, 153). Now, however, upper class Cajuns are the cultural activists who are in a position to prosper from the marketing of the traditions of poorer Cajun society which survived transplantation, developed in Louisiana, or were re-introduced, like Mardi Gras.

Cajun culture is the result of the specific history of their American experience, which includes the racial discord of the Reconstruction era as well as the changing gender roles of our time. The reasons both for the discontinuity of the Cajuns' culture and for the mythical nature of their representation, both in the nineteenth century and today, reflect not their difference from the rest of America, but the quintessential American nature of the experiences of both the traditional and the official cultures of the region.

For scholars like Ancelet, who belongs to the group he studies, the folklore revival of the 1960's must have had special resonance. Christine Balfa, whose father, fiddler Dewey Balfa, is most credited with the surge in popularity of Cajun music over the last few decades, told me that Ancelet's epiphanic moment, which revealed the beauty of his own culture, came during a college year abroad spent in Paris. Walking down a street on the Isle St. Louis, he heard Dewey's music wafting into the street; returning to Louisiana, he became one of the most active and eloquent proponents of Cajun culture. Ancelet's experience echoes that of other American ethnologists with genetic ties to their subjects; not only did he need to see his culture validated from the outside to appreciate it, he also finds himself, perhaps inevitably, in the position of a mediator of his culture for the outside world.

However, while other ethnologists' self-identification with their subjects, Rosaldo for example, have led them to question the relationship between the ethnographer and the culture s/he describes, positing the necessary and desirable subjectivity of the ethnographer, Ancelet maintains a stance of objectivity in his representation of Cajun culture for the consuming public. The glossy cover of *Cajun Country* features a Mardi Gras rider, with painted clown-face and codpiece stuffed with straw, standing on his horse; this presentation surely indicates that this is an "exotic Other." The back cover proclaims the book to be "An encounter with the savory culture of Cajun Louisiana", reproducing the ubiquitous use of Cajun cuisine, especially the mixed-heritage gumbo, as an icon for Cajun culture, which thus becomes a consumable product. While the book is a good compendium of traditional Cajun cultural traits, it is clearly selective in its representation of the group. By choosing not to discuss Cajun culture in the context of their specific history, especially the ways in which Cajuns have been and are the same as their neighbors in southwestern Louisiana, Ancelet reduces his portrait, if not to an emasculated caricature, at best to an invitation to the general public to come and taste this exotic dish.

RURAL FESTIVE CUSTOMS IN EARLY MODERN FRANCE

Tracing the roots of Cajun Mardi Gras leads us back to the Old World. There, we find antecedents of the forms of the Cajun *quête*, but also of the misrepresentations of popular culture that are endemic to traditional ethnology. As in modern times, social tension in early modern France was expressed through festive forms; the attempts to repress these customs, and the indefatigable reassertion of the autonomy of the traditional culture, created a social counterpoint mirroring the class and gender disjunctions that signaled the beginnings of modern society.

There were fifteenth-century fishing expeditions from the northwestern coast of France searching the maritime regions of eastern Canada for Atlantic cod to dry on the beach and ship back to an increasingly famine-threatened Europe. The first group of emigrants from France to settle in the New World were indentured peasants, ancestors of the Cajuns, who were transported to what was then called Acadia, and is now New Brunswick. The name may have come from the Native name for codfish, although some believe it to be a reference to Arcadia, Virgil's utopia. In exchange for a number of years of work for the *seigneur* who financed the enterprise, they were promised land. The original group left the countryside near Loudun, in western France, in 1632; coincidentally, this year in Loudun was marked by a witch trial which eventually drew thousands of spectators to witness the burning of a Catholic priest accused of sorcery.

The wave of witch-trials sweeping Europe at this time, in which the typical defendant was not a priest but a poor peasant woman, was not an isolated problem, nor indeed the worst problem faced by rural communities. Many factors acted as incentives to leave France for the future Acadians to leave France for what would be a difficult new life in the wilderness of Canada. Their very survival in France, tenuous enough because of the seasonal nature of their food supply, was increasingly threatened by a combination of economic and social restrictions, of which the witch trials were an integral element, initiated by the emerging centralized monarchy in Paris and facilitated by its ally the Catholic Church. Traditional rights and liberties which had been enjoyed from time immemorial by the villagers were systematically abridged, as these emerging central powers attempted to broaden their control. This effort touched every aspect of rural as well as urban life, and private as well as public, resulting in the social crisis that is the overwhelming feature of the popular culture of early modern France.

Underlying the disruptive effects of these political and moral reforms was one factor over which no person, not even Louis XIV, had control: the weather conditions. The early modern period was marked by the growth of glaciers in Scandinavia and the Alps, and historians agree that in Europe at this time, cold winters and wet summers resulted in devastating crop failures.

Infestations of ergotism in stored grain which produced ill effects including hallucinations and convulsions, and no doubt provided the stimulus for some of the accusations of sorcery and deaths by fire which were commonplace in this period.

The close connection between the advent of agricultural crises and social unrest is noted by Robert Muchembled, who shows that the times of the "*vaches maigres*" coincide exactly with the peak times of witch-hunting in France.[30] Yet later episodes of famine, war and rising taxes between 1690 and 1713 resulted in only sporadic violence compared with earlier reactions to similar conditions. Historian Yves-Marie Bercé says this is because the people's perception of the taxes had changed; by then, "people had forgotten about violent resistance; the communities and the local independence which encouraged revolt had been worn away. Poverty alone was not enough to drive people to arms."[31] This

---

[30]Robert Muchembled. *Sorcières: justice et société aux seizième et dix-septième siècles.* Paris: Editions Imago, 1987.

[31]Yves-Marie Bercé, *Fête et révolte: des mentalités populaires du XVIe au XVIIIe siècle.* Paris: Hachette, 1976, p. 328.

erosion of the spirit of autonomy that had been a feature of village life reflects the concerted effort of the Church and state to control the formerly isolated rural districts, and an important element of this campaign was the attempted suppression of traditional agricultural holiday celebrations.

Bercé points out that all the *Croquant* uprisings of the seventeenth century occurred in springtime, specifically during festival times like carnival, the first of May, and summer solstice. People also used the traditional forms of these celebrations in their revolts against newly-levied taxes on salt and increases in the price of bread. Bercé argues that the accession of Louis XIV in 1660 marked a turning-point in popular culture, since during the course of that century "a number of festivals or customs thought to be shocking or disruptive died out or were adulterated either because they were prohibited or, simply, because they were forgotten" (335) after the population shifted to urban areas.

The basis of ritual and ceremony in a simple, agricultural society is unambiguous: its goal is to ensure fertility, in people, animals and crops. The agricultural year was marked in rural France by a cycle of festivals celebrating the seasons, from the new year (which was traditionally celebrated in the spring) through midsummer and harvest-time, to the winter solstice feasting that marked the return of the sun. These celebrations, accompanied by communal feasting and drinking, also served the function of socially binding the people of the village together as they relaxed the usual restrictions on behavior. By the early modern period, the Catholic Church had incorporated these agricultural celebrations into its liturgical calendar; this is not to say that some aspects of Christian ideology, for example the birth and the resurrection of Christ, were not themselves originally inspired by seasonal cycles. In any event, the Church has always been ready to adopt indigenous forms into the official practice of the religion, producing notable syncretic features in France like the many local saints who were formerly gods of springs or hills, and the cult of the Virgin Mary which echoes pre-monotheistic, "pagan" fertility worship. Carnival is one of these syncretic festivals, coming as it does at the time of the traditional new year, and incorporating, even today, some features of the original fertility ritual.

According to Arnold Van Gennep, Roger Vaultier and other folklorists who have documented this region, traditional carnival practices in western France also served the related function of regulating and enforcing marriage practices in a given community. Carnival was the time for the newly-married or engaged young people to rule the village; it was the standard time for the *charivaris* to ridicule matches deemed inappropriate by the group because of age discrepancies, as well as second marriages which deprived the community of marriageable young people (and the usual marriage fees). While it is true that this rule of the young can be seen as a temporary role reversal, this aspect of the festive behavior is diminished by the fact that the regulation of sexual behavior was enforced year-round, if necessary, by these youth groups. As we shall see, role reversal, and the topsy-turvy world of carnival, was a *topos* that emerged later, from the increasingly hierarchized society of the cities. The traditional rural carnival was characterized by competitions among young people or between different age groups, and by *quêtes,* forerunners of the Cajun practice. The form of the celebration varied somewhat from place to place, but there is enough consistency in the overall picture to allow us to discern the outlines of the source of the Mardi Gras run (without the horses) as it is practiced by Cajuns in rural Louisiana today.

Carnival marks the passage from winter to spring. The first possible day of Mardi Gras, February 2, coincides with the ancient custom of the "*sortie de l'ours à la Chandeleur,*" the day on which, traditionally, the local bear comes out of hibernation. If the sun shines, the bear will go back into its cave and winter will last forty more days; otherwise, it comes out and spring begins (a custom that survives in the United States as Groundhog's Day). The youth groups, called *bachelleries* and made up of adolescent males, would choose one of their group to be the king of their *royaume de Jeunesse,* either by election or by right of having won a contest involving athletic ability, such as catching a chicken, or killing it by throwing a stick or shooting an arrow. Thus the new king, like the new year, takes over from the old, and the cycle of life and communal order goes on.[32] Although the tradition is dominated by these groups of young men, there are also recorded instances of groups of young women taking part in the festivities, and even engaging in parallel chicken-killing contests to choose a queen in Eperlecques.

Competition is one of the consistent features of rural carnival practice; the obvious function it performs is to identify leaders in a group, as well as to bond the group together. In addition, transferring rivalries to the level of sport is an effective means of diffusing hostility to avoid *actual* bloodshed. The competition was some-times within the youth group, and this is the aspect that has survived in the Cajun tradition of competing to

[32] Martine Grinberg. "Carnival et société urbaine à la fin du XVe siècle" in *Fêtes de la Renaissance, III*, J. Jacquot & E. Konigson, eds. Paris: CNRS, 1972, p. 548.

catch a chicken released by a farmer at a given stop on the Mardi Gras run.

Folklorist Roger Vaultier has collected evidence of these popular festive customs from one of the few types of written record that exist for this period: the letters of remission given by the royal authorities for infractions committed by the rural population, which were preserved in the national archives and detail the crimes sufficiently to give us an idea of the surrounding festivities. Thus a text from the Maine region in 1482 tells us that "'le iiiième jour de ce mois de février auquel jour les enfans de l'escolle avoient entreprins pour parfaire leurs esbatemens de la joute des jaulx d'aller acourir la poulle aux champs, iceulx enfans se misdrent en ung champ' appartenant à un homme qui ne voulut pas qu'on courût la poule sur ses terres d'où une bagarre."[33] Other letters make reference to "toute une série de faits folkloriques

---

[33]Roger Vaultier, *Le folklore pendant la guerre de Cent Ans d'après les Lettres de Rémission du Trésor des Chartres.* Paris: Librairie Guénégaud, 1965, p. 56.

ayant un coq pour acteur, le carnaval et les jours gras pour cadre [en Champagne] où, jusqu'au siècle dernier, les joutes de coqs, les rois de l'école, la course à l'oie avec un bâton, étaient des plaisirs favoris de la jeunesse durant cette période de l'année" (56). Vaultier cites the work of Alcius Ledieu who wrote in 1902 that "'une coûtume qui s'est perpétuée presque jusqu'à nos jours c'est le combat de coqs qui se faisait annuellement, pour le mardi gras, dans les écoles primaires de chaque locali-té de la Picardie. Le possesseur du coq déclaré champi-on était proclamé roi, c'est-à-dire chef de la troupe des écoliers qui se rendait dans chaque maison pour recueillir des oeufs, du lard, ou quelque menue monaie.' Dès le XVe siècle, des pièces d'archives constatent l'ex-istence de cette coutume à Abbeville'" (57), for which a town in southwestern Louisiana is named.

These Mardi Gras competitions, which also fre-quently included games of *soule*, an early form of soccer (58), or of archery (65), fit into the larger scheme of the competition for survival that was integral to village life.

The competition could be among members of the youth group, as we have seen, or between the married and unmarried members of the community (54), or between neighboring villages (58). The significance of the competition emerges from the nature of the economy of the village, which has changed little over the centuries: it is a closed system, with finite resources. In this economic scheme (and with its resulting psychological consequences), one person's gain is necessarily another's loss; in contrast to the pioneer mentality that exists in a society in the process of expansion, there is no independent gain in this economy. Competition in the village environment is part of the overall desire to attract good fortune and prosperity for one's own group, and deflect harm onto one's rivals.

This closed system of bio-economic resources is also reflected in the custom of "killing Carnival" which survived the transition from rural practice to some urban carnival festivities. The destruction of an image (such as a straw figure) identified with the old year, is a symbol of renewal and rebirth. The magic transfer of benefit and harm plays a role in this practice, as noted by the folklorist Arne Runeberg. Drawing on the work of James Frazer, he describes the springtime custom of "carrying out Death" as fastening a straw image representing Death to a pole and carrying it around on a *quête* which is sometimes rewarded with foodstuff, and sometimes met with resistance, as "neighbors would be on the look-out ready to repel the ill-omened figure, so that hard knocks were often exchanged between the two parties. The principle of magical transfer is conspicuous in these customs, whose aim is to get rid of the harmful power with which the image of Death is loaded."[34] The ceremony of killing or carrying out Death (sometimes called in France "*la Vieille*," or old woman), is concluded by burning the figure, tossing it into the water, or throwing it over the boundary of the next village, thus averting misfortune on home grounds. The figure of *la Vieille* re-emerges in urban forms of Carnival, transformed into a

---

[34]Arne Runeberg. *Witches, Demons and Fertility Magic* . Helsingfors, Finland, 1947, p.214.

symbol of the austerity of the Lenten season, and thus an adversary of the fat, male Mardi Gras, as in the 1559 painting by Breugel, the "Combat of Carnival and Lent."

The *quête* is the principal feature of rural French carnival festive forms found in Cajun culture. The underlying logic of the ceremony, which consists of the youth group travelling around to homes in the area to request food for the communal meal and dance which will culminate the festivity, reflects the shortage of food that exists in early spring in any agricultural economy. Those with more resources are encouraged in this way to share with their neighbors, confirming the solidarity of the group.

Arnold Van Gennep, the premier folklorist of the region from which the Cajuns originated, notes that rural forms of Mardi Gras *quêtes* in northern France and Belgium were only loosely organized, and rarely masked, in contrast to the urban festival: "Il semble donc certain que les déguisements et mascarades du Cycle de

Carême et Carnaval sont dans le département du Nord un élément spécialement urbain, mais à aucun degré rural."[35] Van Gennep mentions that although some authors seem to have assumed that rural Carnival celebrants were masked, "en tout cas, ces masques libres, non arrangés en cortèges, ni intégrés dans des processions, faisant une quête pour leur propre compte et ayant le droit d'intriguer, sinon de molester, les passants, d'entrer dans les maisons pour se 'faire reconnaître,' sont folkloriquement antérieurs aux déguisés corporatifs ou processionnels" (142). As in modern-day Louisiana, there is a functional aspect of disguise when retaliatory or other mischief is afoot, and impromptu disguises were used in Cajun Mardi Gras runs before the post-World War II revival of the custom brought more organized masking, borrowing from celebrations in Mobile and New Orleans.

---

[35] Arnold Van Gennep. *Le Folklore de la Flandre et du Hainaut Français*, vol. 1. Paris: Librairie Orientale et Américaine, 1935, p. 141.

Bercé tells us that a number of the annual festivals that made up the cycle of holidays, namely the twelve days of Christmas, Carnival, Easter and the first of May, included this sort of begging tradition, in which the young people went from house to house asking for contributions for a feast, or for small change for items such as candles for the parish church. By the end of the sixteenth century, the authorities began to ban this sort of activity because of the violence and dissolute behavior that was liable to accompany it (Bercé, *Fête et Révolte*, 21).

In the case of popular forms of justice, specifically the charivaris that were under the jurisdiction of the youth groups, changing functions can indicate changing social conditions. As noted in Chapter Three, E.P. Thompson's study of charivaris in early modern England led him to believe that the form of the custom remained static while the function changed. Thompson describes the change of English charivaris from the earlier focus on non-traditional and second marriage partnerships, adultery, and wives who controlled their husbands, to a nineteenth-century focus on wife-beating husbands. He asks, concerning the earlier "skimmington" ritual in which a man whose wife is deemed to "wear the pants" is ridden around town backwards on a mule while being beaten by a cross-dressed male, whether "la prédominance de tels skimmingtons et charivaris semblables en France aux XVIe et XVIIe siècles indiquait la solidité des valeurs de la domination patriarchale, ou au contraire la lutte défensive d'un système qui se sent menacé par une effervescence féminine?" (302). He argues that the more recent focus on wife-beaters is a reflection of the devalorisation of the patriarchal system and the corresponding rise in the status of women. Charivaris not only expressed conflict within the community but also fixed the rules of that conflict, typically limiting actual violence and instead using laughter to resolve communal tension (289). Thus the charivari was an expression of the legitimacy of the people's control over their own sexuality, even as the community's concept of acceptable behavior changed. As such it was a target for the bans which would attempt to substitute official sanctions and procedures for popular justice systems.

Life in the village was democratic, relative to the social structure that was developing in the towns during this period. Although young and poor people as groups were disenfranchised in the urban environment, the transition to the urban society resulted in the biggest changes for women. An agricultural society makes fewer distinctions in gender roles, since important jobs like harvesting require the participation of the entire community. Women gain prestige in the agricultural community by being more intimately involved in the ultimate survival of the group as a result of their management of childbirth, although evidence points to the participation of men as well as women in other healing situations, as is true of modern-day French and Cajun *traiteurs*, or healers. Marriage determined the ownership of land, a vital aspect of rural economy, and Van Gennep mentions that one may perhaps discern "un reste du vieux droit germanique, selon lequel les femmes avaient plus d'autonomie que conformément au droit romain, dans le fait qu'à Steenvoorde et 'dans les villages aux environs de Cassel,' ce n'est pas au père de la jeune fille que la demande (de mariage) est faite par le garçon, mais à sa mère; et que c'est aussi à elle que s'addresse la jeune fille" (78). It appears that marriage arrangement was traditionally a feminine function in agrarian societies of northwestern Europe.

The active role that women played in the rural culture is also evident in their participation in carnival festivities. Groups of young women competed to kill a fowl and become queen of their group. Van Gennep cites the historian Piérart's description of a ceremony in Avesnes "qui faisait intervenir les filles d'une manière qui suggère une signification sexuelle primitive: 'Le jour de Mardi Gras on attelle les demoiselles à un chariot destiné à conduire au haut d'une colline le bois avec lequel on doit brûler *Mardi-Gras*'...Il ajoute que ce jour-là, comme le jour du raccroc de la ducace et à la Sainte-Catherine à peu près partout dans l'arrondissement,

c'était aux jeunes filles à payer les violons du bal et à en-
gager les jeunes hommes à danser" (150-1). Although
this sort of carnivalesque role-reversal can also function
to maintain the status quo, Van Gennep associates the
active courting role of these young women

with the tendency towards broader women's rights in
northern European culture, compared to their more restricted role under Roman law.

The relatively democratic structure of the village
was joined to the villagers' belief in their right to control
their own existence. As Muchembled points out, the festival is the ultimate expression of the peasant culture,
"puisqu'elle réalise, momentanément il est vrai, une sol-
idarité exceptionnelle: maîtrise de l'espace, du temps,
des rapports sociaux, du bonheur tel que peut offrir la
vie." (*CP, 127*). This is why it was so important for the
authorities to ban the festivities, the bonfires, the dances,
the games, the access to taverns: by banning the traditional agrarian festivals, the authorities hoped to cut the

popular culture at its roots. As we shall see in the next chapter, this was not easy to do.

Sexuality of any kind was suspect in the new social and political order. The doctrines established by the Council of Trent preserve the record of the Church's campaign in the mid-sixteenth century to elevate the ethic of celibacy, while attempting to curb even marital sex by restricting popular customs. For example, the Council condemned a Protestant belief that marriage is preferable to virginity or celibacy, and that the regulation of marriage belongs in the civil domain.[36] The most important change resulting from the session of 1563 (which produced the official doctrine of marriage reform) was the legal nullity of any "clandestine" marriage, i.e. one not performed by a priest. These marriages were widespread, since the marriage contract was considered consensual in the medieval period. Marriage was deemed to exist if both parties expressed their consent, with or

---

[36] *Histoire des Conciles Oecuméniques: Trente*, Gervais Dumeige, ed. Paris: Editions de l'Orant, 1981, p. 454.

without the presence of a priest or the consent of their families.

The monarchies of Europe had long been interested in requiring parental consent for marriage, and the doctrine of the Council of Trent established this as a requirement if the marrying individual was under the age of twenty-five (458). The custom of young couples living together during a trial engagement, noted by the folklorist Van Gennep as widespread in the times before the Council of Trent (80), was restricted by the Council's action, and the new canons also banned sex between the newly-weds for a period of three days. Not only did the Council forbid wedding celebrations during the holy periods of the year like Lent, married couples were also supposed to abstain from sex during these times. The Council's doctrine on marriage customs also restricted the number of godparents that a child could have to one godfather, or at the most one godmother as well (464). Church regulation of the most intimate details of private life became part of the initiative to bring the individual under the control of the central powers. Every aspect of these regulations reinforced the vertical power structure that linked the individual to the king and pope through a patriarchal chain, and attempted to diminish the horizontal ties that bound individuals to their smaller groups and villages. The success of this attempt was relative to the urbanization of the public, as the peasant revolts of the marginalized areas demonstrated.

The construction of popular customs as a diabolic plot against the authority of the Church and State provided the theoretical basis for the ongoing attempts to suppress those customs, which ranged from popular justice systems like the charivaris to the practice of traditional healing or ritual magic to control the weather. The one form of popular culture that embraced every aspect of village life perceived by the authorities as threatening was the festival, since, in addition to providing traditional opportunities for libertine sexual practices and popular justice, the festivals kept the people from their work in an era when the cost of foreign wars was straining royal finances. It is no coincidence that, as the attempts to eradicate traditional festivities grew more widespread in early modern Europe, the festival also provided the form for popular revolt.

CARNIVAL FREEDOMS AND PEASANT REVOLTS

As the population in France became more and more concentrated in urban areas, Mardi Gras and other popular festive customs changed, reflecting the social contexts which produced them. The outlawing of specific practices associated with traditional festivals is well-documented, and indeed, as we have seen, is frequently the only surviving documentation of traditional customs associated with the agricultural cycle of *fêtes*. Yet these attempts to control popular expression were countered by the persistent reassertion of traditional autonomy. In some cities, interdictions of festive activities went on for hundreds of years; in Lille, for example, games and dances around the bonfires of the mid-summer feast of St. John were banned as early as 1382, and the bans had been renewed a dozen times by 1601.[37] While this indi-

---

[37]Robert Muchembled, *Culture populaire et culture des élites dans la France modern: Xve-XVIIIe siècle.* Paris: Flammarion, 1978, pp. 197-8.

cates the limited success of the attempts to regulate public behavior, the cumulative effect of the bans was to channel the people's festive energy into more controlled activities like parades, which were modeled after the official processions of the Church and the monarchy.

Control was most effective in the cities, where society evolved as a vertical hierarchy, but the attempted suppression of popular festivities was ongoing in the countryside as well. Muchembled notes that the distribution of officers of the king increased from one in 115 square kilometers and per thousand residents in 1515, to one in ten square kilometers and per seventy-six inhabitants in 1665 (*CP*, 45). In addition to this increased surveillance by the central government, the Counter-reform movement in the Catholic Church enlisted missionaries whose rallies became substitutes for traditional activities. One such preacher, Thomas Connecte, travelled in Belgium and northern France on a mule, and in Arras in 1429 attracted a crowd of thirty to forty thousand people. They were so moved by his sermon against gaming and women's fashions of tall, conical hats and pointed shoes that they made a bonfire of the offending articles of clothing and objects used in games of chance like cards and dice (*CP*, 194). The Franciscan Phillippe Bosquier published his *Sermons sur la parabole du prodige évangélique* in Paris in 1600, containing violent attacks against women. He warned against the traditional festive customs, describing them as diabolical:

> L'idolâtrie étoit pure paillardise en ses
> fêtes et sacrifices comme en ses dieux et
> déesses, desquels je n'en trouve nuls qui ne
> furent ou putiers ou putains... Je n'oseroye
> déboucher en vulgaire les impudicitez des
> festes de Faunus, ny des festes saturnales
> et florales, solemnisées par putains toutes
> nues et par hommes enfarinez de mesme.
> (*CP*, 196)

The salacious tone of this harangue was no doubt designed to help stir the crowd into religious fervor.

The Church and monarchy encouraged this construction of traditional folkways (like bonfires at midsummer) as an organized religion led by Satan, the Anti-Christ, whose goal was to overthrow Christendom.

123

There is no evidence that anything like this ever existed, but the theory provided a justification for the eradication of festive customs, and the privileges and autonomies that accompanied them. Yves Bercé has collected a number of writings which document the attempted suppression of festivals, and their language is borrowed from the doctrine of diabolism. For example, a dean of the cathedral of Senlis in Paris published a speech against the traditions of the *Fête des Rois*, calling it a "maudite et diabolique coutume",[38] and claiming that "Le Démon corrupteur, ce calomniateur universel, a gasté et sally nos plus pures traditions, par des scandales publics, par des débauches legitimées...Les Dimanches qui sont nos jours de Sabath, ne servent qu'à la paresse, ou à la gourmandise, et des artisans et des honestes gens du monde: toutes les festes des Saints s'employent au Culte des idoles, ie veux dire à la satisfaction des passions et des actions de la Chair" (202).

---

[38]Yves Bercé, *Fête et révolte: des mentalités populaires du XVIe au XVIIIe siècle.* Paris: Hachette, 1976, p. 200.

The cult of idols and of the flesh was broadly interpreted by the authorities, and served as a pretext for actions which had a correspondingly pervasive effect on the lives of the populace. An interdiction of popular festivals, specifically the games and other activities of the youth groups in La Rochefoucauld, issued by the Parlement of Paris in 1781, cites earlier *arrêts* from the fifteenth century, and confirms the crown's intention to "faire défense à toutes personnes, de quelqu'état, qualité et condition qu'elles puissent être, de s'assembler ni de s'attrouper, sous quelque prétexte que ce puisse être...pour jetter aucunes personnes dans l'eau, soit pour jouer à la boule, soit pour battre du tambour et danser, soit pour exiger aucunes sommes des personnes qu'ils peuvent rencontrer" (218). The document went on to charge heads of household with the responsibility to control their children and servants, and to forbid merchants to sell wine on Sundays and feast days, during church services, and after eight o'clock in the evening in the winter and ten o'clock in the summer "sous peine de vingt livres d'amende contre les Cabaretiers et Aubergistes, de cinq livres d'amende contre chacun de ceux qui seront trouvés à boire chez eux, du double en cas de récidive, même d'être poursuivis extraordinairement suivant l'exigence des cas..." (219). Thus the authorities relied ever more heavily on official sanctions to attempt to control a population whose restraint had formerly consisted in large part of the accountability of the individual to the commune.

The interdiction of custom was also part of the class struggle that was a feature of the religious reform movement. As Bercé points out, these measures reflect the changing mentality of the upwardly mobile classes, not of the general populace (168). The myths of modernization, of a more enlightened religion and rational philosophy to replace the egalitarian, animistic perspective of the village, carried with them "la condamnation des modes anciennes involontairement conservées par ceux qui restaient à l'écart des courants de développement. Renoncer aux gestes ancestraux, aux danses villageoises, au costume provincial, c'était s'élever dans l'echelle sociale, c'était accéder à la civilisation" (190). This class struggle was exacerbated by the demographic shift to urban areas, since the well-to-do no longer felt obliged to care for the the poor, as they had in feudal times.

A related factor that led to support for the suppression of festivals from the more affluent peasant population was the increasing privatization of land. The communal fields that had formerly been used for bonfires and dances became private property whose owners were concerned with limiting access to the crowds of carnival and St. John's celebrations. In addition, the land-owning peasants employed the poorer agrarian workers, and were interested in limiting the leisure time of their employees in order to increase their productivity. As in the witch trials, the collusion of a significant portion of the population was necessary to explain the widespread nature of the suppression of festival activity which led to the emergence of the new, more controlled urban forms of celebration.

Traditional society insisted on the individual's accountability to the group; its demise, and the violence that ensued, contributed to the banning of traditional practices. For example, in the Loire region in the late sixteenth century, the *quêtes* which played a central role in most of the cycle of traditional feasts (the *Fête des Rois*, Carnival, Easter, May Day) were banned by the authorities, as they became marked by increasingly violent episodes of extortion and vengeance. Despite the convergence of the attention of the authorities on these customs, the old forms were never entirely rooted out, although their significance was necessarily fluid.

Various factors contributed to the spasms of rural flight that changed the demographic face of France during the fifteenth and sixteenth century. Yves-Marie Bercé notes that the hailstorms and rainy weather that destroyed crops for years in a row in some areas forced inhabitants to take to the roads looking for food, some of them returning home when conditions improved, but many taking up permanent residence in the growing urban centers and towns, and others (notably women and children) becoming vagrant.[39] In addition to the bad weather, taxes to support the monarchy's war efforts and requirements to provide food and shelter for troops in the winter contributed to poverty and famine in the countryside. New laws regarding land and water use struck another blow to the sustainability of the agricultural society, challenging the very basis of the peasant culture, their unwritten, unquestioned customary right to the communal use of natural resources. In August 1669, for example, the government issued a celebrated ordinance on waters and forests which imposed harsh restrictions and prohibitions on the gathering of firewood and acorns, and the grazing of pigs and sheep, not only in the forests but in the surrounding moorland (*HPR*, 18), contributing greatly to the hardship of the poorest segment of the population.

---

[39]Yves-Marie Bercé. *History of Peasant Revolts: the Social Origins of Rebellion in Early Modern France*, trans. by Amanda Whitmore. Cambridge: Polity Press, 1990, p. 63.

The peasant revolts against these onslaughts on their traditional rights reflect a clash of cultures, the oral culture and that represented by "the officers of the crown, products of a new law that was written and pre-scriptive, men who demanded evidence and title deeds and grants of land drawn up in good and due form, and who validated their own identity with printed docu-ments bearing an official stamp" (*HPR*, 20). The barrage of orders and decrees from the humanist magistrates and priestly reformers focused on festive traditions. As Ber-cé points out, "authorized, accepted, spontaneous, and constantly indulged in, they were, in their day, the token of an unquestioned solidarity which was felt by the in-habitants of every village and district. Through them the population showed that it thought as one. This popular culture drew its strength from a simultaneous devotion to tradition and excess" (*HPR*, 30). A symbol of com-munal solidarity, festivals provided a ready-made form for the peasant revolts. As the forms of carnival celebra-tions in urban areas changed, the functions of the festi-vals changed as well; however, the changed forms can be recognized as reassertions of the traditional popular autonomy, as well as the sexual energy, that the authorities were attempting to curb.

An example which which presages the evolution of the ritual into an urban affair is found in a description of a *course au chapels* (*chapels* being the wreaths of flowers and ribbons worn by participants) which took place on Mardi Gras in 1586, in the town of Saint-Quentin (Aisne):

> La Jeunesse allait à la messe en cortège, et le "Roi" faisait bénir les chapels par l'officiant. Le cortège, accompagné de mendiants qui réclamaient "largesse," partait jusqu'aux murailles de la cité, hors desquelles se déroulait la course. Le vainqueur était déclaré "roi des chapels" pour un an, et rentrait en ville cérémonieusement, tel un véritable prince...Les échevins invitaient le prince fraîchement promu à un banquet, dans la grande salle du conseil. (Muchembled, *CP*, 178)

In contrast to the village festivities which brought together disparate elements of the community, the hierarchy of the urban festival has well-defined layers: the beggars, who still ask for charity, the youth groups, on their way to becoming militia, the city and church officials who legitimate the procedure, and the audience who watches the spectacle.

In urban carnival festivities, official religious processions held by the town honoring visiting nobility, a royal birth, or an important military victory, relegated the townspeople to the role of spectator; they also provided models for the ironic parodies which began to characterize carnivalesque activity (*CP*, 172). The festivities were typically organized by the Abbeys of Misrule, which had a new role to play in the urban arena. Now based on neighborhood groupings which also reflected occupational groupings, they were charged with keeping the peace during festivals (in addition to their traditional role of enforcing social standards). Official surveillance of the festivals was augmented as well, as they were increasingly taken in hand by the authorities. No longer the winner of a competition, symbolizing the cyclical relinquishing of power to the young, the Mardi Gras monarch in urban parades often representated the empowered segment of society, while the ancient customs survived only on the fringes of society, and in the outlying country districts. Bercé tells us that the *reinages* of the guild festivities "increasingly had to be conducted by auction rather than election. Elections had fostered disorder insofar as the journeymen tended to choose the most boisterous of their number; but auctions were won by well-heeled notables anxious to make their mark with a conspicuous show of largesse" (*HPR*, 31).

Muchembled notes that these devalorized youth groups were often organized along the lines of military models furnished by the companies of archers and *cannoniers* that existed in each town (*CP*, 205). These *Abbayes de Liesse,* which took the place of the youth groups in organizing festival activities, were charged with a new function, to establish good economic relations with neighboring towns; a text from Arras in 1533 describes their function as to "entretenir les anciennes et bonnes

amitiés des villes prochaines (proches) et communication des marchands et autres gens de bien fréquentans en
ceste ville" (*CP*, 181). The order of entrance to the mass
for nineteen titled participants, from Cambrai, Arras,
Douai and Pas-de-Calais, in the last *Abbaye de Liesse* in
Arras, in 1534, is preserved in the town archives, from
the *Prévostes des Coquins* through the *Princes, Admirals,
Cappitaines* and *Abbés*. Presumably local politics decided
the hierarchy in this new form of town rivalry.

Natalie Zemon Davis points out another change
in the role of the neighborhood groupings that made up
the *reinages*:

> The Abbeys also carried on charivaris...in
> circumstances which the village passed
> over in silence. We catch the Abbey of
> the rue Mercière in Lyon planning a pa-
> rade on the ass against a well-off tanner in
> the neighborhood about whose recent
> beating by his wife 'we have made good
> and sufficient inquiry.' This *chevauchée*
> was needed 'in order to repress the temeri-
> ty and audacity of women who beat their
> husbands and of those who would like to
> do so; for according to the provision of di-
> vine and civil law, the wife is subject to

134

the husband; and if husbands suffer themselves to be governed by their wives, they
might as well be led out to pasture.' Any-
way it is the month of May now, the 1517
report goes on, and this season requires
frolics and diversion. Here again we have
the loud and mocking laugh of misrule intended to keep the traditional order. Interestingly enough, while charivaris
against second marriages were central in
country misrule, in the cities charivaris
against dominating women were the most
frequent.[40]

This changing focus of popular justice reflects an important shift in relations between men and women in the
fifteenth and sixteenth centuries, which prefigured a
worsening position of women under French law.

The authority of women eroded as the population moved to urban centers that were more easily
brought under centralized governmental control. Constance Jordan, in her comprehensive study of *Renaissance*

---

[40]Natalie Zemon Davis. "The Reasons of Misrule: Youth Groups
and Charivaris in Sixteenth-Century France," in *Past and Present* 50:
64-65. Oxford: Past and Present Society, 1971.

Feminism,[41] notes that the rights of women of rank to in-
herit property (as well as the offices and income that it
entailed) came under attack after the thirteenth century.
Widowhood had previously bestowed a substantial
amount of power on women, whether it was recognized
by the official (written) culture or not. Increasingly in
France, culminating in the Salic Law of 1464 which de-
nied the throne to women, "new laws superceded customary arrangements that had allowed [women] to function as men economically and even to some extent polit-
ically" (Jordan, 95). By the sixteenth century, most
women in France were prevented by these laws from
inheriting property.

While these changes reinforced the tendency for
urban festive activities to focus on the virago as a threat
to the new public order, the new festive forms sometimes provided, in the persona of the predominant limi-

---

[41] Constance Jordan. *Renaissance Feminism: Literary Texts and Political
Models.* Ithaca: Cornell University Press, 1990.

nal figures, the unruly woman and the fool, models for actual and not merely ritual social criticism and change.

Natalie Zemon Davis argues that the topsy-turvy world of carnival celebration does not always return immediately or permanently to the status quo, but rather experiences real change that persists past the liminal period of time. This is especially true of sexual role-play, because of the constructed nature of gender behavior. But the cross-dressed man or woman is symbolic of broader cultural criticism.

Similarly, cross-dressing and sexual role-inversions in Cajun Mardi Gras, while certainly the legitimate inheritors of age-old sexual tensions, must be considered in both contemporary and historical roles. Like dressing as a Wild Man or a Moor, dressing as a woman historically serves the purpose of liberating the behavior of male carnival revelers. Gender role-play, like the other tropes of the *monde inversé*, has been central to carnival at least since it became an urban phenomenon.

Natalie Davis in "Women on Top" notes that in early modern times, not only were women considered disorderly par excellence, "the disorderliness was founded in physiology...Long before Europeans were asserting flatly that the 'inferiority' of black Africans was innate, rather than the result, say, of climate, they were attributing female 'inferiority' to nature",[42] specifically to the so-called "wandering womb", etymological basis and supposed cause of (female) hysteria, an image which pervades early modern literature. Men dressing as unruly women are still a commonplace of festive behavior, and women dressing as men to gain freedom of action is an equally common theme in folklore.

As Davis notes, "In hierarchical and conflictful societies that loved to reflect on the world-turned-upside-down, the topos of the woman-on-top was one of the most enjoyed. Indeed, sexual inversion--that is, switches

---

[42]Natalie Zemon Davis. *Society and Culture in Early Modern France.* Stanford CA: Stanford University Press, 1965, p. 123.

in sex roles--was a widespread form of cultural play in literature, in art, and in festivity" (129). Davis doesn't dispute the traditional view that a function of this cultural play is a reinforcement of order and stability in the hierarchical society; but, like some of the Iota women, she does posit another dimension to the results of this role-playing, the same sort of multiple significance that characterizes carnival behavior in general.

Davis points out that, in early modern Europe, the relation of the wife (the potentially disorderly woman) to her husband expressed the relation of all subordinates to their superiors (127), not only because the economies of European societies were still tied up with the relationships of feudal service, but also because the emergent monarchies drew upon the model of the family to justify their own rule. In early modern Europe the female was considered the embodiment of disorder; but the unruly woman could be "a multivalent image that could operate, first, to widen behavioral options for women within and even outside marriage, and second, to sanction riot and political disobedience for both men and women in a society that allowed the lower orders few formal means of protest" (131). The most conservative political institution, the family, is touched by play with the woman-on-top image, an enduring societal trope which is rooted in at least a conception of an alternative social structure.

Davis notes that among the "traditions, symbols, and solidarities that legitimated the numerous rural and urban uprisings of early modern Europe…was the carnival right of criticism and mockery, which sometimes tipped over into real rebellion" (147). According to English and some French customary law, women, since they were subject to their husbands' rule, were not legally responsible for their own actions, a legal precedent which encouraged carnivalesque male cross-dressing as a protectionary device. Davis suggests that the female persona represented resistance to official culture not only because it minimized men's responsibility for, and disassociated them somewhat from their actions, but also because "the males drew upon the sexual power and energy of the unruly woman and her license (which they had long assumed at carnival and games) – to promote fertility, to defend the community's interests and standards, and to tell the truth about unjust rule" (150). Thus gender politics became a symbol of class conflict.

The development of social hegemony in the Renaissance was tied to the neo-Platonic aspiration to an intellectual life that could transcend the imperfections of physical life. Faithful to the classical model as elaborated by Aristotle, the dual nature of man, spiritual and physical, was felt to be reflected in the two sexes, of which the male was the higher, spiritual being and the female the incarnation of the *"beste imparfaicte"*. In the western European system of sexual symbolism, the female embodied the disorderliness of Nature; and dressing like women gave men the freedom to indulge in disorder themselves, whether this might be for festive or for political purposes.

The traditional associations of sexual symbolism provided a ready-made pattern for disorderly behavior, regardless of its origins:

> The donning of female clothes by men and the adopting of female titles for riots were surprisingly frequent, beginning (so our still scanty data suggest) in the seventeenth century. In many of these disturbances, the men were trying to protect traditional rights against change; in others, it was the rioters who were pressing for innovation. But in all cases, they were putting ritual and festive inversion to new uses. (147)

Cross-dressing was related to dressing as a "Wildman," a giant, or an African Moor; and playing at being the "cultural Other," be it a woman or a "savage," was a way to be in touch with one's physical nature, which was excluded from the human ideal by neo-Platonism. It was also a way to criticize the existing structure of society, which was based on that philosophy of the ideal: the perfect, the homogenous and therefore the controllable individual. Like the classical story of Phyllis riding Aristotle, symbolizing the unruly woman unmasking the ideal truth, topsy-turvy carnival imagery suggests situations in which "youth overthrows age, and sexual passion, dry sterile philosophy; nature surmounts reason, and the female, the male" (Davis, 136). Unofficially, carnival was an assertion by the demographic majority of their ultimate uncontrollability.

Thus the conflicts between the customs actually practiced by the society and the written code of the official culture had as their subtext the struggle for women's rights; and by the same token, the feminist struggle had as its subtext the questioning of any authority, whether based on divine or natural law, the two traditional sources of patriarchal authority.

As role-reversals and cross-dressing gained importance as themes of patrician urban carnival activities, women were explicitly excluded from active roles in the official parades, as in a 1548 ban in Valenciennes (*CP*, 187), which followed interdictions of 1547 denouncing "les bandes de femmes insensées" which assembled at

143

the festival of St. Christopher as "frivoleux et fort inutile", and leading to "la dérision, bien souvent, de notre sainte religion" (*CP*, 169). Still, the traditional festivities did not disappear easily, as the ongoing nature of the bans testifies. Formally excluded from the official parades, the *menu peuple* continued to use the traditional festive forms to carry on their struggle for existence in the face of worsening conditions.

One of the more famous examples of this is the violence that erupted during Carnival in the late sixteenth century in Romans, a town in the Lyonnais region of France, the events of which were chronicled by historian Emmanuel Le Roy Ladurie.[43] Over a period of several years, carnival activities degenerated into class warfare, as primitively armed peasants, artisans, and nobles waged combat in the streets and outskirts of Roman. Comparing the urban violence to the *reinages* in the villages, Ladurie notes that in Marsas and Chan-

---

[43]Emmanuel Le Roy Ladurie, *Le Carnaval de Romans: de la Chandeleur au mercredi des Cendres 1579-1580*. Paris: Gallimard, 1979.

temerle, "la première réunion frondeuse s'est regroupé à l'occasion des jeux d'hiver; ceux-ci étaient animés par la jeunesse masculine, d'âge militaire et sportif. Ils étaient couronnés par l'election annuelle et canularesque d'un roi d'Epiphanie ou de Carnaval" (112). Stemming from traditional youth group the activities, Ladurie points out that from the institutionalization of the movement to its procurement of arms was a small step.

In the peasant revolts that erupted, especially in border areas such as Poitou where the people had formerly enjoyed a relative freedom from outside taxation and control, we see the ultimate expression of the traditional popular justice of the village against what they perceived as the injustice of the new order. Bercé notes that in the mythology of these revolts, the *Croquants* and the *Tard Avisés* (whose self-given name means "out-of-date") believed they were fighting to re-establish the justice and freedom that was being shattered by state control; new taxes were held to be unwarranted precisely because they were new, and because they eroded the traditional exemptions and privileges from which the border regions had previously benefited. Described by the records as "vagrants and good-for-nothings" or "humble people," the rioters formed the element of society whose hand-to-mouth lifestyle could result in vagrancy following the least misfortune. The targets of the riots were often merchants and "tax farmers," a new breed of entrepreneur whose profits came from the taxes they collected. The peasants believed that the king was robbed and deceived by his ministers, a perception fueled by the fact that the flagrant abuses of the new tax system were never addressed on the official level; instead, popular justice, delivered by the communes through the traditional festive forms, was their only recourse (227).

Bercé tells us that "the most constant element in these riots was the presence of women. At night on the high roads there were women armed with stones who even took part in the peasant ambushes. Aldermen noticed the presence of women carrying swords and halberds in the crowd which ran riot in Poitiers. Some of the crowds in our survey, six out of thirty-one, were even made up exclusively of women. They yelled, threw stones, broke into shops and plundered the grain. This flocking of women to the riots at the price of bread is a reminder of the almost biological nature of this kind of episode. Bread riots were the most spontaneous and essential of all types of rebellion--but also the most short-lived and the easiest to disperse" (174-5). While we may question Bercé's assignment of a "biological" nature to the bread riots because of the "flocking" of women that is a feature of this form of protest, we can appreciate the fact that the price of bread would have been of primary concern to the women in the community, who were en-trusted with the preparation and presentation of food for their families. Failing to catch a merchant who had managed to get away from the crowd in an incident in 1709, "the women of Saint-Jean-d'Angély went and took down a dried-up skeleton from the local gibbet, and stuck it in front of (his) door. In Limoges in 1714, the grain merchants had satirical songs made up about them and were derided in the streets. They were painted in effigy like criminals who had been sentenced to death *in absentia*, and a baying mob took the dummies through the town and burnt them in a public square" (173). However, women's participation in peasant rebellions was not limited to the bread riots.

For example, in a tax riot at Angoulême in 1629, "'the people decided to put the women in command. The women gave orders like captains, surrounded by armed bodyguards. In May 1705 the houses sheltering a number of excisemen were set on fire in Limoges. The arsonists turned out to have been 'a large number of women, girls and children sprung from the dregs of the common people. Their husbands and fathers played no part in the riot at all'" (222). These tax riots were more planned than the spontaneous bread riots, and included the use of disguises such as comic masks, and cross-dressing among the men. Many of these riots broke out on holidays; the tax agents, instructed to maintain heightened vigilance because of the smuggling that took place during festival times, were sometimes chased from the fairgrounds with mock toasts. Rioters also performed charivaris on taxmen, riding them through town like cuckolds, festivals which could end in killings: "at Barbezieux in 1636 the offending excisemen were thrown in the river. At Marennes in 1644 they were torn to pieces by the crowd" (41); clearly this sort of violence invited further control by the officials, and further motivation for them to provide spectacles to divert carnival energy into acceptable channels.

Still, the authorities recognized the need for recreation among the people; describing the social functions of carnival and other festivities that expressed the lower class's antagonism towards the upper class, Mikhail Bakhtin in *Rabelais and His World*, quotes a circular letter of the Paris School of Theology in 1444 which was intended as an apology for the Feast of Fools, a festival which ridiculed church rituals and symbols. The letter reveals the Church's perception of the benefits it could realize by allowing the people to enjoy this sort of play:

> Wine barrels burst if from time to
> time we do not open them and let in some
> air. All of us men are barrels poorly put
> together, which would burst from the
> wine of wisdom, if this wine remains in a
> state of constant fermentation of piousness
> and fear of God. We must give it air in
> order not to let it spoil. This is why we
> permit folly on certain days so that we
> may later return with greater zeal to the
> service of God.[44]

The motivation for official support of carnival celebrations has changed little in five hundred years; for example, in present-day New Orleans, Black groups calling themselves the "Mardi Gras Indians" spend the whole year preparing the elaborate costumes they wear for the carnival parade, diverting them from their habitually adverse economic and social situation.

The fact that the ritual role-reversal of carnival serves as a safety-valve for dissipating the societal pressures of the lower classes, thereby ensuring and propagating the hierarchical status quo during the rest of the

---

[44]Mikhail Bakhtin, *Rabelais and his World*, translated by Helene Iswolsky. Cambridge, Mass., 1968, p. 75.

year, does not negate the actual empowerment that people feel as a result of the ceremonial play.

Although these role-inversions are temporary, in early modern Europe they often lasted several months of the year, between Christmas and Easter; and the effects of carnival actions do not always go away overnight. They are therapeutic for people, letting them laugh at the powers that be. As a rite of spring, carnival affirms and celebrates the renewal of the natural world and the survival and regeneration of the people, mocking the ultimately ephemeral nature of "officialdom." François Rabelais captured the Renaissance spirit of the carnivalesque, and his narratives reflect the social disjunctions of his time. Drawing on the tradition of carnival, he uses androgynous imagery to reveal the underlying indeterminacy of meaning that throws into doubt the Renaissance construction of reality.

THE CARNIVALESQUE IMAGERY OF
FRANÇOIS RABELAIS

Radical changes swept Europe during the lifetime of François Rabelais: the printing press facilitated the centralization of political power, paper money destabilized the economy, and women struggled against their own devaluation in the urban arena. Rabelais' narratives raise questions of the legitimacy of this centralized control which converge with the question of the indeterminacy of meaning of experiential reality, proving Rabelais a modern writer. Literary extensions of the popular tradition of carnival criticism, his novels parody established authority and celebrate the popular voice.

The androgyny and reversed gender roles that we find in Rabelais, radical symbols in his era, represent an interrogation of the patriarchal order, including the commodification of women inherent in the marriage exchange which was the basis of the European cultural economy. Like the Renaissance feminists for whom the cultural relativity of gender identity, as distinct from sexual identity, was an important argument for women's rights, gender role-play in Rabelais is linked to his other representations of the indeterminacy of meaning of signs, visual and otherwise, which inherently challenge the social hierarchy. More typical of the popular culture than of the official culture of Renaissance Europe, androgyny in Rabelais may be seen as a celebration of the unofficial power of the disenfranchised, especially women.

Yet literary critics have commonly found, in the themes and images of François Rabelais, an absence of the feminine voice, if not an outright misogyny. Ironically, the misogynist message found in Rabelais by androcentric interpretation reproduces the misinterpretations of the signs of the Other that Rabelais criticizes in his parodies. One might even say that the conventional perception of Rabelais, as a writer whose quasi-obscene representations of women signify his anti-feminism, has been marked by a selective critical memory that sees grotesque images of female genitalia as signifying differently than parallel male grotesquerie. Rabelais's grotesque is androgynous, like the walls of Paris which Panurge describes to Pantagruel as built of intersticed female and male genitalia[45]; traditional criticism has tended to ignore this androgyny. Feminist critics have recently begun to explore alternative readings of Rabelais which recognize the richness of meaning indicated by androgyny, and in doing so explain some of seeming paradoxes of his narratives. Rabelais addresses the problematic assumption of objectivity of western philosophy: the indeterminate signs that we give and are given must be interpreted reciprocally through a lens of experiential reality. In Rabelais' text, women do speak, but are not understood by men; and the explicitness of this message, combined with the parodic nature of Rabelais' work, makes it a self-deconstructing text, meant to be read as if in a mirror reflecting the perspective of Otherness.

---

[45] François Rabelais, *Pantagruel*. Paris, 1972, p. 409.

Christine de Pizan provided the feminist model for reading misogynist texts in her *Book of the City of Women* (1404-05), pointing out that "one can interpret them according to the grammatical figure of *antiphrasis*, which means...that if you call something bad, in fact, it is good, and also vice versa."[46] When we apply this method to Rabelais, many instances in the narrative which exhibit a surface exclusion of the feminine voice reveal an ironic twist. In the *Tiers Livre*, for example, the heroes of Rabelais' parodic quest seek words and other signs from fools and women, but misinterpret them because of their failure to transcend their own perspective; and their quest for knowledge, which in Rabelais's world is situated in the outsiders of society, is ultimately doomed by this failure. The androgyny that is the basis of the carnivalesque in Rabelais suggests that a richer, fuller reading of life's indeterminate text requires an effort, at least, to consider life from different perspectives

---

[46]The quotation is from the translation by Earl Jeffrey Richards. New York, NY: 1982, p. 7.

than one's own. Far from excluding women from his work, Rabelais eloquently represents their commodification and voicelessness, and, like the Renaissance feminists, suggests that a recognition of the cultural relativism of gender roles is fundamental to a multidimensional understanding of relations, political and otherwise, between the sexes.

Yet Rabelais' interrogation of patriarchal control, transparent enough when he mocks clerics and scholastics, has eluded traditional criticism when it comes to the "woman question." The *Tiers Livre* has been seen by most critics as the clearest expression of Rabelais' misogyny, and indeed even as a negative contribution to the *querelle des femmes*. This literal reading of Rabelais' text to demonstrate his anti-feminism ignores the parodic nature of his work; the topsy-turvy world that Rabelais invokes in this book demands, instead, Christine de Pizan's reading *au rebours*. Thus inspired, we can see that reading Rabelais from the perspective of otherness makes the unfaithful reader's alternative interpretation, ironically, more faithful to the spirit of his text than a "faithful" acceptance of its apparent anti-feminism.

Rabelais invites an alternative reading of his novels from the first words of the prologue to Pantagruel. He addresses his reading audience as "Très illustres et très chevaleureux champions, gentilz hommes *et autres*" (my italics), thus effectively dividing society into the haves and have-nots. It is the gentlemen, we feel, who, having read the *Grandes Chroniques* of Gargantua, "comme vrays fidèles, les avez creues gualantement" (Prologue, 31). "The others" are unfaithful readers, including a female or otherwise marginal audience, whom Rabelais suggests will approach the text with a certain skepticism, which may be inherent in their alterity. The ensuing fantastic tales are proof enough that the unfaithful reader, who questions the surface reality of the narrative, is faithful to the spirit of Rabelais.

In the *Tiers Livre*, Rabelais addresses women more directly, since the book is dedicated to Marguerite de Navarre, an important feminist contributor to the *querelle des femmes*. However, the storyline revolves around the problematic fidelity of women, specifically of the future wife of the trickster Panurge, thus intimating that a woman would be an unfaithful reader, and that the authorial father could not trust her to produce an interpretation that is faithful to his seed of meaning. Yet Rabelais dedicates the work to this unfaithful reader; as Elizabeth Chesney Zegura argues,

> Rabelais has woven the possibility of this reversed feminist reading into the fabric of the text, equating sexuality with textuality and using the cuckolding woman as a metaphor for the unfaithful reader. When viewed through a woman's eyes, the stereotypic misogyny emerges as a specular satire of men, and this alternative reading is further supported by the unfaithful narrator, whose vacillation between phallic and effeminate voices serves to interrogate the myths of androcentric culture.[47]

---

[47] Elizabeth Chesney Zegura, "Towards a feminist reading of Rabelais," in *Journal of Medieval and Renaissance Studies*, 15 (1985) I, p. 126.

The storyline also questions the underlying economy of wife exchange, as Rabelais puts in doubt the value of women as bearers of true economic wealth (i.e., legitimate heirs). The text is presented as the child of the author, and lack of authorial control is conflated with lack of fatherly control; thus the question is not only of the legitimacy of children, but also of the legitimacy (and efficacy) of patriarchal authority.[48] But it is the consistent misperceptions of women by men that provide the humor in the most famously "misogynist" episodes of Rabelais' novels, and not just in the *Tiers Livre*.

For example, in Chapter 15 of Pantagruel, Panurge follows his description of the Parisian walls, constructed from the economical Parisian callibistrys and bracquemars, with a sort of fable introduced as taking place "au temps que les bestes parloyent (il n'y a pas troys jours)" (P 15:211). In the story, a lion frightens a woman in the forest and, recently wounded by a

---

[48]See Carla Frecerro, *Father Figures: geneology and narrative structure in Rabelais*. Ithaca, NY: Cornell University Press, 1991.

woodsman's axe himself, on seeing her exposed private parts, perceives her to have been wounded in this way as well; and, "considerant son comment à nom, dist: 'O pauvre femme, qui t'a ainsi blessée?'" (211). The lion fetches a fox, and exhorts him to keep flies from the woman's blessed "wound," saying that "Dieu t'a bien pourveu de quehue; tu l'as grande et grosse à l'advenant; esmouche fort et ne t'ennuye poinct" (213). The grotesque description of the unnameable and unknowable female genitalia is, of course, the focus of the joke; but the joke seems to be on the boys who don't understand what they see, or, more tellingly, don't know what to do with their own sexual equipment. Rather than an exposure of woman's fallen state, a feminist interpretation can read in this farce an exposure of male foibles.

In an episode in the *Quart Livre* similar to this one in its grotesque analogy of the vagina as a wound inflicted by a male aggressor, an old farmer's wife tricks a devil, who has challenged her husband to a scratching contest, into believing that her vagina is a wound made by her husband's fingernails, thus saving the family's harvest. The "petit diable" who afflicts the couple, and all the other unfortunate residents of the Isle of Papefigues, has required a share of their harvest, like an absentee landlord, "depuys l'heure et le temps qu'au Pape vous feistez la figue" (QL XLV:207). Ironically, the devil is thus an agent of the Church, an allusion to the widespread selling of pardons by the clergy in Rabelais' time.

However, the devil's inexperience leads to his demise. His unfamiliarity with agriculture production leads him to be tricked by one "laboureur": the man agrees to give the devil his choice of shares in the harvest, when it is divided into the above-ground and below-ground yield, and the devil chooses the worthless portion both times. When the old farmer's wife frightens away the devil with her trickery, she takes advantage of the devil's similar inexperience with human reproduction, again suggesting an analogy between the devil and the clergy. This Rabelaisian woman, using the limited resources which are encompassed in her own body to outsmart the authorities, is clearly a female trickster. As Elizabeth Zegura and Marcel Tetel point out of the "vieille" and the devil,

> she has sold him a line, using marketplace craftiness to inflate the value of her husband's fingernails and devalorize the devil's claws. This triumph of female ingenuity lends an intriguing symmetry to the episode, reminding us that a woman's breach of epistemological taboos is the biblical source of original sin. Wilier and less pious than her husband, who chooses to pray and pay penance rather than fight, this new Eve uses the "fruit" of her apostasy--an agile mind--to outsmart the devil, thereby saving her family and removing the yoke of intellectual repression.[49]

Here is a trickster to rival Panurge himself, who saves her husband and her property through her actions.

At the end of *Gargantua*, the giant king builds an abbey for his companion, Frére Jean, who was instrumental in the king's recent victory over the Picrocholes.

---

[49]Elizabeth Chesney Zegura and Marcel Tetel, *Rabelais Revisited*. Twayne Publishers, New York, NY: 1993, p. 145.

This utopian Abbey of Theleme, which invites all to "Cy entrez," seems to represent a feminist vision like de Pisan's *Le livre de la cité des dames*, hypothesizing the equitable gender roles to which the Renaissance feminists aspired. The women are mirror images of the men, different only in style of dress and in their manual occupations; otherwise, "Tant noblement estoient apprins qu'ils n'estoit entre eulx celluy ne celle qui ne sceut lire, escripre, chanter, jouer d'instrumens harmonieux, parler de cinq et six langaiges, et en iceulx composer tant en carme, que en oraison solue" (G 57:429). Yet this "reflective" woman can only serve to reinforce the status quo, since she requires the same degree of privilege as her male counterpart. The Thélémites' marriages are described as idyllically as their educations, for "si bien avoient vescu à Theleme en devotion et amitié, encores mieulx la continuoient ilz en marriaige: d'autant s'entreaymoient ilz à la fin de leurs jours comme le premier de leurs nopces" (429). This fairy-tale ending to the vision is followed immediately by a poem which is the text of "un enigme qui fut trouvé aux fondemens de l'abbaye en une grande lame de bronze" (G 42:429), the enigma upon which the Abbey is founded and which closes *Gargantua* on a typically Rabelaisian note of ambiguity.

Ironically, this description of a utopia in which the sexes enjoy an equity of privilege is followed chronologically by the seemingly anti-feminist *Tiers Livre*. In this book, Panurge, the modern anti-hero, replaces Pantagruel as the focus of the narrative, as he leads the prince and his companions on a parodic epic quest for the answer to the "woman question," which as framed by Panurge is a negative interrogation of the sexual fidelity of women. This narrative line has historically been interpreted at face value as a negative contribution to the *querelle des femmes,* which paints all women with the same broad brush of infidelity and greed. However, the fact that Panurge receives positive answers to the question of whether he would be cuckolded by his future wife must be seen in the context of his own character.

While Panurge has "un puce à l'oreille" to marry, he is concerned that he will marry an adulterous wife; in the course of the *Tiers Livre*, various marginal figures are sought to prophesize concerning this question, including fools and female oracles. Their responses are interpreted by Pantagruel, and everyone else in the company except Panurge, as an affirmation of Panurge's fear that, if he marries, he will indeed be cuckolded and otherwise mistreated by his wife. Yet this narrative seems less an indictment of the nature of women in general than a confirmation of Panurge's own nature. Panurge's framing of the question of the character of women holds its own answer, since an honest woman wouldn't want him; his verbal trickery, in persistently putting a positive spin on the negative responses he receives from the authorities he consults, confirms this analysis. Panurge's question posits his future wife as a mirror image of himself, but one which ironically reflects his true nature; in other words, Panurge fears, with good reason, that he will marry a female trickster and become a "trickster tricked," a well-known topos in folk humor. By transferring the quest for the Word and the Holy Grail from the epic hero and prince Pantagruel to the trickster Panurge, whose unknown lineage makes problematic his concern with the legitimacy of the children of his marriage, Rabelais turns the woman question upside-down. His parody of the *querelle des femmes* not only does not denigrate women (any more than the rest of mortal kind), it puts the entire patriarchal order in doubt, since illegitimacy undermines the value of the patriarch's estate in the most fundamental way.

Questions of illegitimacy have already provided the comic deconstruction, earlier in Rabelais' work, of the elaborate geneologies of the giants as well, since their race, according to the Bible, was the result of an adulterous union between the sons of God and the daughters of men.[50] The royal giants represent the upper-class' desire to sustain, not only the purity of bloodlines, but also the economic model of marriages ar-

---

[50]Walter Stevens, *Giants in Those Days: Folklore, Ancient History, and Nationalism.* Lincoln, NE: 1989.

ranged to benefit family interests. Gargantua returns from the dead, in the *Tiers Livre*, to deliver a royal interpretation of the philosopher Trouillogan's response to Panurge's question, "'Me doibs je marier ou non?' (Trouillogan) avoit respondu: 'Tous les deux ensemblement'; à la seconde foys, avoit dict: 'Ne l'un ne l'autre'. Panurge se complainct de telles repugnantes et contradictoires responses et proteste n'y entendre rien. 'Je l'entends (dist Gargantua) en mon avis. La response est semblable à ce que dist un ancien philosophe, interrogé s'il avoit quelque femme qu'on nommoit. Je l'ay (dist il) amie; mais elle ne me a mie; je la possède, d'elle ne suys possedé.'"(*TL*, 35:427). Gargantua's interpretation reiterates the economic model of marriage which is documented as far back as Aristotle; and Pantagruel, heir to the patriarchy, seems content to leave the question of his marriage to Gargantua, to be arranged after his return from the quest. His gigantic feats nearly disappear from the narrative, as the action in the later works revolves around Panurge, a very different sort of protagonist.

Panurge is presented from the first as a trickster. Pantagruel, a student in Paris, meets him just after he receives a letter from his father which parodies the precepts of a humanist education. At the scene of their encounter, Panurge replies to Pantagruel's greeting in a handful of contemporary, archaic, and invented languages, displaying a linguistic ability the utility of which is put in doubt as his message (that he is starving for food) remains obscure until he responds in French (P, 9:143). Panurge is the anti-hero who contributes to Pantagruel's instruction in the ways of the world, serving as an object lesson in how not to behave, yet prospering in spite of his unethical behavior.

When cleverness is not enough, the trickster of oral tradition is prepared to transgress accepted ethical behavior in order to win; he differs in this way from the epic hero, like Pantagruel, whose ethical code is more important than the outcome of his adventure, whose success derives from his inherent superiority, and whose appeal is to the upper classes. Tricksters in folk literature are traditionally the heroes of the underclass, like Jack the Giant Killer and Puss-in-Boots, whose cleverness, especially their linguistic ability, help them to overcome more powerful opponents. These characters move across society's borders using carnivalesque strategies. The trickster god Anansi of western African mythology, antecedent of the Br'er Rabbit of African-American folktales, is androgynous, representing the ambiguities of meaning found in life. Panurge exhibits this gender role-play, discarding his gender-specific *braguette,* or codpiece, at the beginning of his marriage quest, and replacing it with an ambiguous robe resembling a monk's habit (the joke here revolving around the celibacy and thus ambiguous sexuality of the clerics).

With Panurge as the hero of this parodic quest, the outcome is already put in doubt; himself a representation of the indeterminacy of meaning, Panurge's inability to transcend his own perspective dooms his quest. Already established as an inveterate womanizer, he consults his friend Pantagruel first for advice on whether or not he should marry, asking for reassurance that his wife will be faithful to him. In a comic sequence of conflicting answers based on Panurge's phrasing of the question, Pantagruel suggests that he will get what he deserves, saying, "Point doncques ne vous mariez, car la sentence de Senecque est veritable hors toute exception: ce qu'à aultruy tu auras faict, soys certain qu'aultruy te fera" (TL 9:161). Panurge rejects this answer, as he will all the other negative predictions for his marriage which he receives during the quest.

Having offered Panurge a great deal of contradictory advice drawn from classical literary authorities, Pantagruel advises him that, "Puysque, par les responses des saiges, n'estez à plein satisfaict, conseillez-vous à quelque fol" (TL 37:445). As Zegura points out, this quest ultimately leads the Utopians "to a woman: either the oracle of Bacbuc or Panurge's future wife, both pivotal rather than terminal figures whose responses, if voiced, would turn the quest back on itself" (TFR, 126). The fool, whose oracle must be interpreted in the mirror of Otherness, is woman; the source of the ultimate failure of Panurge's quest for knowledge of the female Other is his continuing misinterpretation of the messages which women give him.

The sybil of Panzoult is the most explicit example of this. The ancient woman is sought by Panurge and company, who believe that she is the oracle spoken of by Homer. Epistemon fears that they will not get a response from her, because they do not have "le rameau d'or" that Aeneas needed to enter the underworld, a symbol which associates the phallus with economic exchange. Panurge, however, is equipped with "une couille de belier pleine de carolus nouvellement forgez" which he gives the sybil along with food, drink and a gold ring engraved with a toad, an animal associated with witchcraft. She uses the pieces of gold in her carnivalesque ritual, in which she ties a shoe on her head "comme les presbtres mettent leurs amict quand ils voulent messe chanter," and consults burning sticks before delivering her prophecy:

Adonques s'escria espovantablement,
sonnant entre les dens quelque mots bar-
bares et d'estrange termination; de mode
que Panurge dist à Epistemon: suys
charmé; elle ne parle poinct christian...A
quelle fin fredonne elle des babines
comme un cinge demembrant escrevisse?
Les aureilles me cornent, il m'est advis
que je oy Proserpine bruyante: les diables
bien toust en place sortiront. O les laydes
bestes! Fuyons. Serpe Dieu, je meurs de
paour...Adieu, ma Dame, grand mercy de
vos biens. Je ne me mariray poinct, non.
Je y renonce dès à present comme alors.
(TL 42:243)

The sybil's prophecy for his marriage prospects thus seems clearly understood by Panurge at the time, even though he claims not to know her pagan language. Yet, when she writes the future of his marriage on leaves of a tree and tosses them to the wind, the oracle's message becomes, like any written word, subject to interpretation. Pantagruel interprets the enigmatic verse that they piece together from the scattered leaves negatively, but Panurge persists in his failure to transcend his own needs, and insists that the written message prophesies a faithful wife. The woman's words, whose meaning is felt forcefully in her presence, when fixed on leaves (of paper) are distorted in this parody of androcentric interpretation.

As the epic quest of the *Tiers Livre*, whose goal is purportedly to reassure Pantagruel and his masculine company of the legitimacy of their paternity, and thus of patriarchal control over women, is continued in the *Quart Livre*, it breaks down into fragmented, bizarre episodes of the company's adventures in strange lands. The far-flung islands which they visit have been charted for the royal court by Xenomanes, "le grand voyageur et traverseur des voyes perilleuses...Icelluy pour certaines et bonnes causes, avoit à Gargantua laissé et signé en sa grande et universelle Hydrographie, la routte qu'ilz tiendroient visitans l'oracle de la dive Bouteille Bacbuc" (QL 1:57). The quest as continued thus references Cartier's and other European explorers' descriptions of exotic worlds; the parodic nature of the work suggests a modern realization on Rabelais' part of the problem of Eurocentric interpretations of the cultures of indigenous people, as reflected in descriptions of newly "discovered" regions by European explorers in proto-anthropological travel stories.

The carnivalesque, and the sexual ambiguity inherent in carnival imagery, become explicit in this, the final book which is ascribed with any certainty to Rabelais. While they make brief visits to many of the exotic islands, the companions most prolonged adventures take place on two neighboring islands which are the site of an ongoing war. The first is the island of Tapinois, its name indicating a site of dissimulation (*en tapinois*: en cachette). Its ruler is Quaresmeprenant, whose name means Mardi Gras, but who is characterized as representative of Lent, only the first in a series of ambiguities surrounding the episode.

While Quaresmeprenant observes the dietary restrictions of Lent (the necessity of which had been reaffirmed by the Church at the Council of Trent in 1547), he is more noted for excess than for austerity, thus representing hypocrisy. Xenomanes describes him as "un grand avalleur de pois gris, un grand cacquerotier, un grand preneur de Taulpes, un grand boteleur de foin, un demy geant à poil follet et double tonsure, extraict de Lanternoys, bien grand Lanternier," his excesses thus associated with the clergy as well as with homosexuality; he is even a "fouetteur de petits enfants" (QL 29:156). In another irony, Quaresmeprenant is a manufacturer and marketer of skewers for fat meat, an occupation seemingly at odds with his religious convictions. When the company learns that Quaresmeprenant's "enemies mortelles," the "Andouilles farfelues...contre lesquelles il a guerre sempiternelle" (157) are female, Frère Jan's reaction is to defend the Sausages, asking "Quel desordre est ce en nature faire guerre contre les femmes?" (158), another reference to the *querelle des femmes*. Panurge, however, considers it foolhardy to be caught between the two camps, and urges a quick departure; but they do not leave before Xenomanes delivers a lengthy anatomical description of the semi-giant, which includes descriptions of genitalia that range from "couilles, comme une guedoufle" (*guedoufle*: bouteille) to "genitoires, comme un rabot" (*rabot*: rave), an appearance of androgyny reinforced by his "mammelles, comme un cornet à bouquin" (QL 31:162-3). This ambiguous sexuality is shared with his ancient enemies, the Andouilles.

The Andouilles' domain is the neighboring island Farouche, whose name clearly evokes the untamed, savage cultural Other. They are described as being sausages from the waist down, but despite their phallic appearance, the Andouilles are identified as female; in an additional touch of androgyny, their queen is named Niphleseph, which is Hebrew for "male member." Following their departure from Tapinois, the Pantagruelists are chased by a whale, continuing the Lenten seafood theme in a topsy-turvy way, as a fish nearly eats them. They succeed in killing the whale, and land on the Andouilles' island to divide it up with an intent to sell the valuable oil of its kidneys, "laquelle disoient estre fort utile et necessaire à la guerison de certaine maladie, qu'ils nommoient Faulte d'argent" (QL 35:175); instead of feasting on the whale, the company's interests have shifted to profitting from its sale.

When the Utopians land on their island, the Andouilles mistake Pantagruel for Quaresmeprenant, presumably because of his size, but possibly also because, as a representative of official culture, and indeed a neo-colonial exploiter of their natural resources, he actually was an opponent of their popular culture. Nevertheless, it is due to this misinterpretation of their motives that the Utopians are drawn, against their will, into a battle with the Sausages. The Andouilles, whom Xenomanes characterizes as "tous jours doubles et traistresses" (QL 36:178), approach the company as if to welcome them, but in fact plan an ambush. At this point in the story, the narrator confuses the identity of the Andouilles even further, on the pretext of defending the veracity of his outlandish tale. Citing the authority of visual evidence, as preserved by written accounts, he addresses his readers:

Vous truphez [:mocquer] ici Beuveurs, et
ne croyez que ainsi soit en verité comme
je vous raconte. Je ne sçaurois que vous
en faire. Croyez le, si voulez: si ne voulez, allez y veoir. Mais je sçay bien ce que
je veidz. Ce feut en l'isle Farouche. Je la
vous nomme...Iceulx toutesfoy n'estoient
que Andouilles pour la moitié du corps,
ou Serpens que je ne mente. Le serpens
qui tenta Eve estoit andouillicque: ce
nonobstant est de luy escript, qu'il estoit
fin et cauteleux sus tous aultres animans.
Aussi sont Andouilles.

Encores maintient on en certaines Acad-
emies que ce tentateur estoit l'andouille
nommée Ithyphalle, en laquelle feut jadis
transformé le bon messer Priapus grand
tentateur des femmes par les paradis en
Grec, ce sont Jardins en François. (QL
38:187)

Thus the "cunning" Andouilles are actually the
old androgynous gods, evoking both Eve and Priapus
(the snake in the Garden whom Rabelais identifies as
having Andouillique ancestry), the old order evoked by
Carnival celebrations and other popular ritual. However, as Zegura and Tetel point out, "as symbols of both
the forbidden knowledge Panurge seeks and of the rich
culinary and intellectual diet upon which Pantagruel

was raised, the sausages are indeed 'traitors,' albeit un-witting ones, when they attack the friendly Utopians, their most ardent devotees" (RR,142).   The names of the Pantagruel's military leaders, Riflandouille and Tail-leboudin, however, suggest that it is simply the fate of the Andouilles to be sliced to pieces, as they are by Pan-tagruel's army of cooks, as part of their life cycle. Rein-forcing this interpretation, the god of the Sausage peo-ple, the flying pig named Mardi Gras, rains mustard on the decimated Andouilles and their allies, the Boudins, and "resurrects the fallen, phallic Andouilles in a tri-umph of reproduction and regeneration. This sausage miracle, which improves upon Christ's miracle of the fishes, suggests that Carnival even more than Lent is di-vinely ordained" (RR,142).

Following this resurrection, Pantagruel meets with Niphleseth; she acknowledges her fault in attacking him, and sends her daughter with an entourage to Gar-gantua, who in turn sends her to the royal court in Paris, like some Oriental princess. Pantagruel gives Niphleseth a knife, and receives from her the story of their ancestor, the pig Mardi Gras, from whom the Andouilles "feurent extraictes," and its healing mustard, "leur Sangreal et Bausme celeste: duquel mettant quelque peu dedans les playes des Andouilles terrassées, en bien peu de temps les navrées guerissoient, les mortes resuscitoient" (QL 42:198). On this note of the "Dead Man Revived," a carnivalesque revival traditionally effected with wine, the Utopians leave "l'isle Farouche."

A fifth book exists, although the authorship is in doubt, in which the travelers actually find the female oracle of the Holy Grail/Dive Bouteille; she delivers to Pantagruel and company the message (to) "Trink", an exhortation which seems unfailing in Rabelais. However, the last verified word of Rabelais was not intended to finish the adventures of Panurge and Pantagruel, for the author in his "Ancien Prologue du Quart Livre" of 1548 reminds his readers that he had asked them at the beginning of the *Tiers Livre* to reserve their laughter for the seventy-eighth book. The unfinished nature of the quest,

which doubtlessly reflects Rabelais' need to keep producing literature to fulfill his economic needs, also reflects
his modern consciousness.

An alternative reading of Rabelais, faithful to the
carnivalesque spirit of his stories, can yield a complexity
that transcends a traditional, misogynist reading. As
Elizabeth Zegura notes, the sexual inversion of the *Quart
Livre*

> may be interpreted negatively as a func-
> tion of the world-upside-down motif, as a
> paranoic reaction of the male to an an-
> drogynous reality that threatens his myth-
> ical supremacy. Panurge certainly is
> afraid. But one can also interpret this in-
> version positively, as a joyous exploration
> of androgyny and castration, for once the
> woodcutter recognizes his lost axe for
> what it was, or plain wood, he reaps re-
> turns in silver and gold. (134)

In the context of the importance to the emergent Renaissance feminism of the concepts of androgyny and the
cultural relativity of gender roles, Rabelais' carnivalesque imagery may be seen as an interrogation, not

only of the institutions of Church and state, but also of the patriarchal structures upon which those institutions were built.

Yet the underlying theme which subtends Rabelais' play with gender roles is the ambiguity of experiential reality, and especially of a written text; it is here, in this indeterminacy of meaning of a text, that connections exist between the ambivalence and androgyny of Rabelais' images and the popular culture of early modern Europe. Western Europe evolved slowly into a literate culture; early modern European culture, although newly possessed of the printing press, was still largely illiterate.

Henry Louis Gates, discussing the primarily oral literature of African-Americans, notes that "text" is etymologically derived from the past participle of "texere," meaning "to weave." Nevertheless, he concludes, "when we 'literates' use the term, we conceive of 'text' by analogy, as a writing, and a written text is 'fixed, boxed-off, isolated,' underscoring 'the chirographic base of logic.'"[51] The tension between oral culture's flexible and interpretive sense of meaning and written culture's sense of meaning as fixed and objective marked the Renaissance, and still exists in contemporary societies.

Gates relates that in western African texts used for divination, and believed to be given to the Yoruba people by the androgynous god Esu, the interpretive principles underscore their open-endedness, which included archaic words unknown even to the interpreter-priests who memorized these texts (26). He argues that this self-conscious indeterminacy of meaning of a text is a defining feature of an oral tradition.

The writing of Rabelais, who was adept in a number of linguistic traditions, reflects these opposing tendencies of the still-strong orality of traditional culture and the new aesthetic of fixed meaning to which literate

---

[51]Henry Louis Gates, Jr., *The Signifying Monkey*. Oxford, 1988, p. 26.

Renaissance men aspired. With his absurd copiousness, parodying the blasons of the poets and the "véritable récits" of early modern explorers, and with his grotesque stories about giants, François Rabelais challenges us to find any fixed meaning in his texts; seemingly the perfect skeptic, he laughs at the idea of "knowing" what language means, or even of knowing that we don't know what it means. Rabelais, a man who perhaps realized that his world had arrived at a multi-sectioned crossroads, and that the search for a unified meaning which characterized the Renaissance would be futile, offers us no answers, but rather riddles. Reading Rabelais, we may be like the Pantagruelistes, who toward the end of their final adventure come across frozen (written? uninterpreted?) words which, the rigor of the winter having passed, thawed and were heard, "nous y veimes des motz de gueule, des motz de sinople, des motz de azur, des motz de sable, des motz dorez. Les quelz estre quelque peu eschauffez entre nos mains fondoient,

comme neiges, et les oyons realement. Mais ne les en-
tendions."[52]

The ambivalence of Rabelais' carnival-esque
imagery thus shares its indeterminacy of meaning with
language itself, and androgynous imagery throws into
doubt not only gender roles, but all social hierarchies
and indeed the constructed meaning of society itself.

Festivals punctuated and defined peoples' lives in
early modern France, as they still do all over the world
in our time. As people adapt to new environments, the
forms of the festivities change to reflect the subtleties of
the societies that produce them. These festive customs
are clues to the tensions inherent in human society, both
in the specifics of their practice and in their interpretation by the various participants, spectators, and authorities who create the many layers of meaning of carnival.

---

[52] François Rabelais, *Le Quart Livre.* Paris, 1993, p. 245.

CONCLUSION

This work developed in an exploratory manner, spreading out from its original focus on Cajun Mardi Gras to encompass the history of cultural studies, and the changing models of that discipline. Along the way, it became less polemic; instead of what I had imagined to be high walls between the academy and its objects of study, I found, as in carnival society itself, permeable borders. The fact that an anthropologist presents her work to her colleagues in a form they can recognize, and which reflects her own subjectivity, doesn't diminish the fact that the fieldwork and the research have had an impact on the lives of researcher and persons of a given culture.

A valid description of a culture not one's own is, simply, the account of one's encounter with that culture, although again that description is a text to be interpreted by another subject. I have tried to integrate my personal experience of three consecutive Mardi Gras celebrations in southwestern Louisiana with the history of Cajun folk culture, and of Cajun society as it exists in America today. The research I did into this history convinced me that the Cajuns' culture is less a product of their roots in early modern France than it is of their intermingling with other ethnic groups in Louisiana.

Yet folklorists cling to the problematic purity of Cajun culture. The representation of Cajun Mardi Gras as a remnant of French culture, for instance, is only partially true; and the profits of cultural tourism can be seen to be a factor in determining what, for the purposes of the "official" view, is authentic. Those who represent Cajun culture to the world are acting as promoters, rather than explicators, of the culture, although historians are more transparent. It would be interesting to explore the connections between the Ku Klux Klan and its acknowledged antecedent, the *charivaris* of early modern Europe. A nineteenth century photo in a history of the Klan shocked me by its resemblance of their costumes to the appearance of the Cajun Mardi Gras today.

Politics has played a part in culture studies since its inception; clearly the idea of ethnic purity, as demonstrated by the purity of cultural artifacts, is appealing not only to those who hope to preserve archaic traditions from the onslaught of the mass culture of the affluent societies, but also to those whose careers depend on the difference between themselves and their subjects. Historically, collectors of popular music, for example, have been notoriously bad about compensating the people upon whose music they establish their reputations.

More than this, representations of folk culture depend historically on the fact of their being seen as static and monolithic; as compared to modern society, folk cultures have been seen by the folk establishment not only as fixed, but as "backward" cultures in need of fixing. In this view, there would seem to be no place for the contemporary practitioner of folk traditions in the United States; yet such traditions exist and are not isolated from the ubiquitous manipulations of public taste that rule our economy.

Tracing the roots of Cajun Mardi Gras to rural France in the mid-seventeenth century, I discovered an historical coincidence that I haven't seen mentioned elsewhere. The original Acadians were indentured French laborers who were obliged to work for several years for the *seigneur* who had financed the settlement in exchange for land in what is now New Brunswick, Canada, but was then a cod-fishing ground for the French. In 1632, the same year those laborers left the area around Loudun, France, there was a famous witch trial in that town, which led to a reformist priest being burned in front of a large crowd. There doesn't seem to be much of a connection between the two events; still, that discovery drew me to the social phenomenon of the witch trials of that time, which were wide-spread in Europe, flaring like epidemics here and there over several hundred years. The processes used at these trials were derived from the earlier Inquisitions in Spain and southern France, but instead of Jews, Muslims or radical Christian sects, most of the victims of the witch hunt were older peasant women, often widowed, some of whom had training in traditional herbal remedies. These trials were symptomatic of underlying tensions in early modern society.

The growing urbanization of France at that time resulted in a struggle between the existing power structures of villages and the expanding central government, which authorized judges and medical doctors from Paris to censure more than just the usual practice of herbal medicine or ritual magic (pins in a wax figure, a knot in a string to cause impotence), but to regulate every aspect, however intimate, of a person's life. The Catholic Church was hardly separate from the monarchy at this time, but the Councils of Trent in the sixteenth century, banning common law marriage and divorce practices which had previously been recognized as binding, and prohibiting sexual relations even between married couples during certain periods of the calendar, exacerbated the progressive loss of individual rights that characterizes this era.

Some of the peasants who struggled to survive in early modern Europe rose up to protest the hardships of escalating taxes, imposed by the throne to finance the wars of expansion that guaranteed France a place among the super-powers of Europe. Women, who lost legal stature during this time, were prominent in the peasant revolts; and men dressed as women were equally common. Dressing as the Other excites possibility; masking hides identity, and the traditional carnival license for mayhem has not only incited revolt, but also provided a form of social protest and a satirical and joyous transcendence of quotidian existence. Bringing into the open a counterpoint to the power of established authorities is the essence of carnival.

Radical changes swept through Europe during the lifetime of François Rabelais: the printing press facilitated the centralization of political power, paper money destabilized the economy, and women struggled against their own devaluation in the urban arena. Rabelais' narratives cast doubt upon the legitimacy of centralized

control, a fact which converges with the ultimate indeterminacy of meaning of experiential reality, and proves
him a modern writer. As a literary extension of the
popular tradition of carnival criticism, his work parodies
established authority and celebrates the popular voice.

The androgyny and reversed gender roles that
we find in Rabelais, radical symbols in his era, represent
an interrogation of the patriarchal order. Like the Renaissance feminists for whom the cultural relativity of
gender identity, as distinct from sexual identity, was an
important argument for women's rights, gender role-
playing in Rabelais is linked to his other representations
of the indeterminacy of the meaning of signs, visual and
otherwise, which inherently challenge the social hierarchy.

Yet literary critics have commonly found, in the
themes and images of François Rabelais, an absence of
the feminine voice, if not an outright misogyny. Ironically, the misogynist message found in Rabelais by andro-

centric interpretation reproduces the misinterpretations of the signs of the Other that Rabelais criticizes in his parodies. Rabelais's grotesque is androgynous, like the walls of Paris which Panurge describes to Pantagruel as built of intersticed female and male genitalia. Traditional criticism has tended to ignore this androgyny, but alternative readings of Rabelais yield richer, more diverse meanings in his texts. In the same way, mainstream interpretations of the Cajun culture tend to ignore the full spectrum of experience that has informed their culture. A topsy-turvy reading of Cajun Mardi Gras reveals it to be a many-faceted experience, signifying differently for different people.

We live in the continuation of Rabelais's modern age; some might call it post-modern, and there is no doubt that communication systems have accelerated the contraction of our global village. This leads to the conclusion that festive customs reflect tensions in various cultures within their specific contexts, as they provide a link to the past. This ambivalence in turn reflects the subjective nature of experiential reality.

AUTHOR'S BIOGRAPHY

Jennifer Cleland was born in Arlington, VA in 1951. Her family moved to Europe in 1962, where they lived in Paris and in Stuttgart, Germany. During the 70's, Jenny played with the Highwoods Stringband, touring on three continents and receiving a Grammy nomination for an album recorded at Carnegie Hall. She received a Ph.D. in Romance Studies from Cornell University in 1999 with her thesis *Cajun Carnival: American Myths and Radical Roots*, and lives in Ithaca, New York.

Jennifer authored *Sage Hall: Experiments in Coeducation and Preservation at Cornell University* with her husband, Robert P. Stundtner, in 2011. The book tells the story of the women's residence, built in 1874, which made coeducation at Cornell possible. The history of the building reflects the early feminist movement in upstate New York, and the social reformism of the founders of the University. The book also relates the controversial 1996-98 transformation of the building, which completely gutted the dilapidated interior while retaining the historic brick exterior walls. The story of the authors' courtship is woven into the narrative of the challenging renovation project, which was managed by the coauthor. For more information, and to purchase books, please visit our web site at www.sagehallbook.com.